A Woman's Guide to Soulful Living

To Sheila,
May Your Life Be
Filled with Peace + Joy,
Anita
4/2005

A Woman's Guide to Soulful Living

Seven Keys to Life and Work Success

Anita Davis-DeFoe, Ph.D.

iUniverse, Inc.
New York Lincoln Shanghai

A Woman's Guide to Soulful Living
Seven Keys to Life and Work Success

Copyright © 2005 by Anita Davis DeFoe

All rights reserved. No part of this book may be used or reproduced by any means, graphic, electronic, or mechanical, including photocopying, recording, taping or by any information storage retrieval system without the written permission of the publisher except in the case of brief quotations embodied in critical articles and reviews.

iUniverse books may be ordered through booksellers or by contacting:

iUniverse
2021 Pine Lake Road, Suite 100
Lincoln, NE 68512
www.iuniverse.com
1-800-Authors (1-800-288-4677)

ISBN: 0-595-34240-X

Printed in the United States of America

Acknowledgement

To women everywhere as you seek to know and understand "self," as you strive to live a life filled with personal fulfillment, as you dare to embrace all of your personal possibilities, I salute you!!!

To my mother, the words on these pages are written in your honor, for you were a woman of intelligence, beauty and grace; a woman who has championed my every dream, a woman who has taught me to have vision and faith, and without question to constantly and earnestly seek more; I salute you!!

To my father, for me you have always been an encourager, a support, a solid rock on which I could stand and hold on to no matter what; I salute you!!

To my husband Griffin, my family, my four dearest friends, Valerie, Linda, Beth and Columbus, through your support and encouragement, you have given me the desire to discover my gifts and talents, a keen interest in pursuing my passion to uplift others, and the courage to persevere no matter what; I salute you!!

To my countless teachers, you have come in many forms, sharing your unique experiences and generously giving me your different perspectives. My teachers have been those who are just beginning the journey and do not know, to those who have journeyed quite some time and now know and understand; I salute you!!!

Finding the road to inner peace and personal joy is not without circumstance. It is a road we must decide to choose because by not pursuing this journey our lives become filled with constant compromise and disappointment. It is not up to us to determine our gifts and our calling; it is up to us to discover it.

Discover your true potential and embrace all of your possibilities because in the end what you get is a reflection of what you have become.

Wisdom......................Harmony

Introduction

I do not know about you, but for me, on more occasions than I would like to remember, the ups and downs, the struggles and strife, the pain and sorrows of life seemed to be getting me down. My mind, body and spirit stayed in constant turmoil, more times than I would like to admit.

Of course when in the public eye, the company of others, I would plaster a mask on my face, paint on a smile and pretend that everything in my world was just fine. But girl, in those quiet moments when it was just me and my thoughts; and my thoughts would not allow me to run and hide, sadly I would admit to myself that nothing in my life seemed to be going right, none of it made much sense. Often, at times, I felt powerless to change my direction and I felt stuck. I even began to feel as though perhaps negative outside and unseen forces controlled my life. Even though deep down inside I knew that this was not true, and clearly understood that I had personal power and control, I still felt as though I was floundering.

For years I made presentations in the United States and in the Caribbean, always telling others how to go about living life as they genuinely seek; how to discover their potential and use their talents to achieve personal success; how to rebound from rejection, disappointment, and failure; and how to experience joy daily in their lives. Many times as I spoke, the personal drama going on in my own life was the basis for the talk I was giving.

Mind you, I understand that challenges are just one aspect of the human experience, and I realize that it is through struggle that we grow and achieve. But for so long, I was certain that women can choose how we respond to our experiences, and we can certainly choose how we allow these experiences to shape our expectations and our actions. This revelation may come easy for some of us, but realization of such a life and attitudinal change is probably more of a challenge for most. For me, discovering how to refocus and reshape my life began to dominate my thoughts on a daily basis, and it still does as I continue my life's journey.

I am not quite sure when or why it happened; maybe it was just a matter of personal growth, or the development of a deeper consciousness. Whatever the stimulant, I am grateful. Grateful because this dissatisfaction, this gnawing deep within caused me to search for, thirst for, hunger for a more personally fulfilling and joyful life. This need to live a better, more spiritually inspired life was the catalyst that led to the writing of this book.

I have always been one to stand up for others, particularly the downtrodden, the disenfranchised, for those who needed lots of personal support and most definitely an encouraging word. I thought one day as I watched the vibrant sun set over the Caribbean Sea, I am always standing up for others; perhaps it is time that I stand up for me.

Deciding to live soulfully takes courage and daily persistence. Deciding to live soulfully must become a personal choice. It must become a core value; an attitude, a belief that true serenity can be a part of one's life.

It is so easy to live for and through others, and for women this can happen so quickly, very subtly. Before we know what has happened, we no longer recognize ourselves. The reflection in the mirror, your reflection, becomes that of a stranger, a woman that you do not even know any longer.

Women by the sheer virtue of our giving, loving and nurturing natures tend to put ourselves last. We assume roles, all kinds of roles in the home, in our families, in relationships and in the workplace. Roles that become quite comfortable to us. Before we realize it, we have put our hopes, dreams; our divine talents on the shelves to collect dust. Far too many of us do not realize that by failing to love, develop and nurture ourselves, it becomes more difficult to give and share healthy love with others.

As we look around, we come in contact with women on a daily basis who exhibit a personal state of tranquility that we envy and seek for ourselves. These women will tell you that the first step to living soulfully is to be true to "self", they will tell you that personal joy comes from learning to rejoice in everything that makes you unique; they will tell you that joyful living comes from making life choices and decisions that come from your values, your heart and your soul.

As many of you are reading this, you are probably saying to yourself; there is nothing wrong with my life, I am already living soulfully. You might be saying one or more of the following: I have a beautiful house, a nice car, a job, wonderful children, a man that I love, and the list may go on and on.

Even if that is the case, you still may not be living soulfully, you may not be truly contented. There could be countless things that you can do to make your life even more fulfilling. Too often there is confusion about the differences between material worth and self-worth. Having and being are entirely two different things, and bring totally different kinds of satisfaction to our lives. A woman must honestly respond to the question, "How Am I Living?"

For most of us, we have yet to satisfy our spiritual yearnings; for most of us there are still numerous opportunities for us to grow. Daily we are reminded that very seldom can external things quench our internal thirst. Hence, this points to a need to dig deeper, to peel back the layers until we uncover our very core, our spiritual center.

In a world where the external rules, living soulfully can be more difficult than one might think. Living soulfully can be the key that unlocks the gateway to your divine talent, your true self. Living soulfully can help you to define your purpose in life and help you to develop your full potential.

What is soulful living?

Seeking and embracing your divine possibilities, your true self

Opening your mind to identify your life's purpose, dreams and calling

Uncovering, understanding and developing your true potential

Listening and loving all aspects of your spirit and personal being as your grew

Finding personal fulfillment, balance and daily joy through your experiences

Unlocking your gateway to personal abundance and spiritual renewal

Living your life with respect, resourcefulness, resilience and without mental limitations

You will find that, "A Women's Guide to Soulful Living: Seven Keys to Life and Work Success" is a toolkit, a resource book, pearls of wisdom designed to help you live a life filled with more joy. This book offers activities and food for thought both designed to nourish the soul in your quest to uncover and become the real you.

I will share with you seven keys that I have found to be critical in a woman's life; seven keys that can increase personal growth and understanding, and can bring more joy into a woman's life. Daily I continue to seek, to learn, to grow; to live the life that my spirit beckons me to live, and I want to share these keys with you so that you too can begin living a more heartfelt life.

Use this book as you will; use it to create peace and personal fulfillment in your life, use it to encourage yourself to achieve more. Do not despair if it seems as though your journey will never end. The journey to know and enrich "self" can and should last a lifetime. The magic of this journey is not gained by completing the trip swiftly and then announcing that your work is done. The magic lies in relishing this spiritual exploration; carving out a personal path that meets your unique needs and honors your divine talents, fully enjoying the experiences that will ultimately help you to embrace all of your infinite possibilities.

Yearn to know, accept and encourage yourself. Strive to find your own personal pathway to inner harmony, genuine serenity and joy. Let's learn to live soulfully my sisters; let's begin the journey today.

Anita Davis-DeFoe 2004

Greatness

Abundance

FOR SOULFUL WOMEN EVERYWHERE

Peace

Life Transformation

Contents

Introduction vii

Introspection 11

1. Who Are You? 14
2. Your Seven Circles of Life 20
3. Check Your Attitude 24
4. The Three Realizations of Life 30
5. Sister, What Cha Gonna B? 35
6. The Gifts of Self 38
7. Become Spiritually Aware 41

Vision 45

1. Hey, Where Are You Going? 51
2. You Better Recognize 57
3. Ponder Phenomenal Potential 61
4. Go for the Goal 65
5. A Matter of Choice 68
6. No Buts About It 71
7. Its At The Door 72

Habits 75

1. Life Patterns 80
2. Destiny Habits 83
3. Delightfully Disciplined 86
4. Finding Balance 88
5. Stopping Self-Sabotage 89
6. Developing Diamond Habits 92
7. Learn the Lesson 94

Relationships 97

1. Relationships Do Matter 100
2. Relationship Readiness 103
3. Accepting People As They Are 107
4. Feeling Your Heart 110
5. Saying I Do To Your Soul 112
6. The Power of Forgiveness 113
7. Do You Hear What I Am Saying 115

Faith 117

1. Following An Invisible Trail Home 120
2. Hold On…It's Coming 122
3. And This Too Shall Pass 124
4. Go On 127
5. You Can Make It Happen If You Only Believe 130

6. Digging Deeper 132

7. Inner Trust 135

Courage..137

1. Be Not Discouraged 140

2. Boundless 144

3. Confronting Fear 147

4. Present…Moment to Moment 152

5. The "Ah Ha" Moment 154

6. Finding Courage To Be You 157

7. Sister, Do The Dash 158

Resiliency 163

1. The Resiliency Factor 166

2. Begin Again and Again 171

3. Everything Must Change 172

4. Pursue the Opportunity in the Obstacle 174

5. Failure is not Final 177

6. Choose Happiness 180

7. Becoming Emotionally Intelligent....................................182

Inner Peace
Purpose
harmony
tranquility
compassion

Joy

Serenity
resiliency
persistence
boundless
balance

focus
dreams
heal
perform
faith

determination
grow

goals
belief
passion
motivation
learn

And so the journey begins………

Are You Ready??
Is Soulful Living For You??

Find out if you are ready to live fully, completely, embracing all of your possibilities; let's begin this journey with a check-up, let's determine if you are really in touch with your soul. Please answer each question honestly responding with a Yes or No.

The Soulful Check-Up

Self-Awareness

1. Do you know and accept both your strengths and opportunities for improvement?
Yes_____ No_____

2. Do you encourage yourself through positive self-talk avoiding excessive personal criticism? Yes_____ No_____

3. Do you feel capable of achieving your goals and dreams? Yes_____ No_____

4. Do you suffer from self-sabotaging behaviors that impede your progress
Yes_____ No_____

5. Do you fear failure? Yes_____ No_____

6. Do you face your problems and find solutions to meet your needs?
Yes_____ No_____

7. Do you feel comfortable giving and receiving compliments?
Yes_____ No_____

8. Do you truly believe that you deserve happiness, success and personal joy?
Yes_____ No_____

9. Do you pamper yourself or do something that you enjoy at least once a week?
Yes_____ No_____

10. Do you have your own definition for personal success? Yes_____ No_____

11. Do you make your own decisions, set your own standards and refuse to allow the opinions of family and friends change your mind? Yes_____ No_____

12. Are you still affected and angry about any past hurts and disappointments?
Yes____ No____

Personal Vision

13. Have you identified your gifts and talents? Yes____ No____

14. Have you created a vision for your life? Yes____ No____

15. Have you developed a personal purpose and does that guide your actions?
Yes____ No____

16. Do you have specific goals that you want to achieve and have you written them down? Yes____ No____

17. Have you prepared a plan to reach your goals? Yes____ No____

Personal Well-Being

18. Do you work in a career that you enjoy? Yes____ No____

19. Do you eat healthy on a daily basis? Yes____ No____

20. Do you exercise at least three times per week? Yes____ No____

21. Have you created a personal financial plan and are you following it?
Yes____ No____

22. Do you openly express your feelings to family and friends?
Yes____ No____

23. Do you have a spiritual foundation that helps you face and overcome personal challenges? Yes____ No____

24. Do you involve yourself in self-improvement activities on a monthly basis?
Yes____ No____

Personal Relationships

25. Are you able to establish and maintain good relationships with family and friends? Yes____ No____

26. Do you have a positive relationship with your mate or with members of the opposite sex? Yes____ No____

27. Are you able to function effectively with co-workers or on teams at work? Yes____ No____

28. Do you allow circumstances from past romantic relationships affect your current attitudes and behaviors? Yes____ No____

29. Do you have unresolved issues with a family member or from a past relationship? Yes____ No____

30. Do you feel complete with or without a romantic relationship in your life? Yes____ No____

31. Do you clearly express your needs and wants when in a romantic relationship? Yes____ No____

32. Would you go to a party or out to dinner alone? Yes____ No____

Personal Growth

33. Do you allow past failures to keep you from pursuing your dreams? Yes____ No____

34. Have you identified the changes that you want to make in your life? Yes____ No____

35. Do you embrace change with a positive attitude and without ongoing regret? Yes____ No____

36. Are you able to rebound from personal setbacks and persist toward your goals? Yes____ No____

37. Do you know the things that you fear and are you working to face these fears? Yes____ No____

38. Have you forgiven yourself for past mistakes and moved on with your life without clinging to these past experiences? Yes____ No____

39. Do you ever procrastinate?   Yes____ No____

40. Are you living the life that you truly desire?   Yes____ No____

Scoring: Give yourself 3 points for each "Yes". Total your points.

Your Score:_____

Here's what your score means:

100—120: You are already leading a life that is filled with purpose, a life that is focused on your personal goals and dreams. You are certainly ready to create a life that brings you even more personal fulfillment. Think about developing some stretch goals for yourself; these are goals that truly incorporate your personal interests and natural talents, goals that focus your efforts on your passions even more. Review your responses and identify those areas that you need to address. You are on your way to soulful living!!!!

75—100: You are almost there. You still have some issues that you need to work on so that your life can become more fulfilling. Review your responses and determine the specific areas that you need to work on improving. Clearly identify your personal goals and create a plan of action that you can stick with daily. For the next 60 days work on these issues, and then re-take the test. Living soulfully is within your reach.

Below 75: There are a considerable number of issues that you need to resolve. Now is the time to honestly evaluate the direction that your life is headed; now is the time to heal old hurts, let anger and disappointment go, and begin to develop both a health relationship with yourself, as well as with others. Look at your career and see if you are doing work that you enjoy. Are your relationships fulfilling or are you holding on out of habit? Only you can take the steps necessary to make your life more fulfilling, but before you can do that you must first honestly acknowledge the things that you need to change. A soulful life can be yours if you want it; creating a life filled with inner peace is simply a matter of choice.

Notes:_____
_____
_____
_____
_____

Things I Need To Do To Live More Soulfully

My Top Ten Self-Defeating Beliefs, Feeling, Attitudes

Based upon your responses to "The Soul Check-Up," list ten beliefs or attitudes that you feel may be holding you back. Identify strategies you can use to change these behaviors. Once you acknowledge your challenges, you can successfully overcome them.

Belief, Feeling or Attitude	How does it affect your life?	How will you change this to improve your life?
1.		
2.		
3.		
4.		
5.		
6.		
7.		
8.		
9.		
10.		

I will live soulfully,
Self-discovery I will pursue.

I will live soulfully,
I will live consciously and to myself I will be true.

I will live soulfully,
My gifts and talents I will use.

I will live soulfully,
I will strive to maintain a positive attitude.

I will live soulfully,
Failure is not final and I will always try.

I will live soulfully,
I will spread my wings and I am gonna fly.

I will live soulfully,
Challenge will unlock the door to my heartfelt goals.

I will live soulfully,
I will totally embrace and nurture my unique soul.

I will live soulfully,
A life of purpose I will lead.

I will live soulfully,
Inner peace and fulfillment are my creed.

A Woman's Guide to Soulful Living

The Seven Keys

Introspection

THE FIRST KEY TO SOULFUL LIVING

The journey to living a joyful, gratifying and exhilarating life begins with introspection.

What is introspection? Introspection is a honest examination of one's thoughts, feelings, attitudes and beliefs. Introspection is searching one's heart and gaining an understanding and acceptance of what is found there. Self-questioning, self-awareness, and self-reflection are the key elements of introspection, and through introspection you will learn to understand, encourage and champion yourself.

Most of us spend tremendous amounts of energy getting to know others, learning aspects of other folk's personalities, their motivations and needs, only to put very little focus on becoming comfortable in our own skins. Until we as women learn to celebrate and honor ourselves, our ability to fully enjoy our lives and the people in it is severely compromised.

As women, we must have the courage to travel down the path to self-discovery, for as we journey, we are certain to uncover the personal treasures waiting for us in the garden of life. Knowing, accepting and loving self are critical to creating the life that you desire, finding the inner peace that you seek, and achieving the level of personal development that you want. There are so many treasures buried inside your soul, but it is up to you to discover them, release them and share them with the world.

Our lives are much like a beautiful flower garden; we decide the things that are planted in our gardens. The soil from which our personal flower gardens grow are our values, our attitudes, and our personal beliefs. With any garden, if it is well tended and nurtured, it will grow and flourish, eventually becoming a spectacular display of color, a blend of exotic fragrances. While if a garden is left unattended; it quickly becomes overtaken by weeds, and these weeds ultimately overshadow the beauty of the flowers, if any of the flowers are able to survive. Far too many of us have forgotten all about our gardens. Many of us no longer appreciate the beauty of our personal spheres. Some of us have stopped nurturing the one thing that we should always hold dear, and that is our own souls, our personal spirits, our selves.

Sister, Sister......how does your garden grow!!!

"A Woman Who Does Not Tend Her Garden Will Suffer From Want"

Key One Introspection

1. Who Are You?

Women around the globe are always focused on and are anxious to improve their circumstances, but how many of us are willing to or actually take the time to go about the business of actively improving ourselves. Ongoing self-assessment is the foundation to continuous personal growth, and this all begins with self-awareness.

For some of us, self-awareness can be an extremely difficult feat to achieve, difficult because we refuse to take an honest look at ourselves or because the circumstances of our lives have made it hard for us to clearly see who we are or what we have become. Until you take the time to earnestly examine your attitudes, values and beliefs, you will find yourself caught up in a vicious circle, unable to free yourself from the psychological and spiritual chains that bind you.

Women by our very nature have a deep desire for people to like us and to love us. Our nature is to nurture and our emotions impact us in countless ways. We spend a tremendous amount of energy on nurturing others, tending to put ourselves last. While contributing to the joy and happiness of others is a noteworthy attribute, being a people pleaser can be a dangerous tightrope to walk if you are not in touch with yourself. No one can hope to totally please everyone all of the time. The expectations and wants of other people change as swiftly as the ebbing tide, so making that feat your goal is simply asking for a life filled with self-doubt. Trying to become the person that you think other people will like turns into a merry-go-round that before long you will not know how to get off.

Our childhood experiences, family and friends serve to shape our earliest visions of the world, but it is up to us to take these moments in time and from them construct our own personalities, our very own value systems, our attitudes. A woman must grow to know and define herself because if she does not, she is prone to make constant attempts to be what others say that she should become. Without this sense of self, a woman will try to fit in, imitate or create a persona that she thinks will be pleasing to others. In the absence of clearly knowing herself, a woman will find herself in a constant whirlwind trying to constantly meet the expectations of those she feels set the standards. Living a life trying to be what you think others would have you be is an extremely difficult assignment, an assignment that most women will find difficult to complete with any measure of success.

I do not know about you, but for me, learning to understand and accept myself has not been easy. Internally, I have found myself pulled in numerous directions in an attempt to please others, to be liked, to fit in. It was when I realized that often when I did or acted as others wanted me to be, even then their behaviors did not change or they still seem displeased with me. I then came to understand that I had to learn how to be me. Daily, I work to get better acquainted with myself, and believe me, when you finally get off the merry-go-round, pull up a chair, sit down and spend some time with yourself, you will be pleasantly amazed by just how special you are.

Knowing who you are makes it so much easier to decide where you want to go in life, and just how you are going to get there. If you do not know who you are, you may try to become what others tell you to be, or be unclear about how to use your talents to bring personal fulfillment into your life. So on a daily basis ask yourself who and what am I becoming? This is a critical aspect of personal introspection, because what we get out of life is intimately linked to who we think we are as a person.

Choosing to become your authentic self is the foundation for a joyous life. Once you decide to step into and get comfortable in your own skin, this self-awareness enables a woman to better create a vision for her life, ultimately opening the door for her to go out and achieve that vision.

Exercise One   Who Are You??????????????????

Answer this question 20 times. Do not answer this question by responding with what you do or what you have. Focus on your characteristics, your attributes; your talents. Answer this question by telling yourself who you really are.

I AM:

Do You Know Who You Are?

Which Mask Do You Wear???

Mask # 1—Busyness
Mask #2—What Will Other People Think
Mask #3—I'm Not Good Enough
Mask #4—Fear
Mask # 5—The Having Syndrome

Exercise Two   What Do You Value????

Values…values are the things that are most important to you. You are your values, so your values should be based upon the things that you hold dear, not what you have or what your friends, family, television commercials or stereotypes say that you should deem important. Do you know who you are and what you value or are you working hard to be what you think others want you to be? Are you wearing a mask?

I Value………………	Why??

Exercise Three   I AM

Create a personal profile about yourself. Write your name in the center of the circle, and then write as many words as you can think of that describe you right now in each of the seven areas listed. Remember your "I AM" circle will constantly change in relationship to your continuous personal growth.

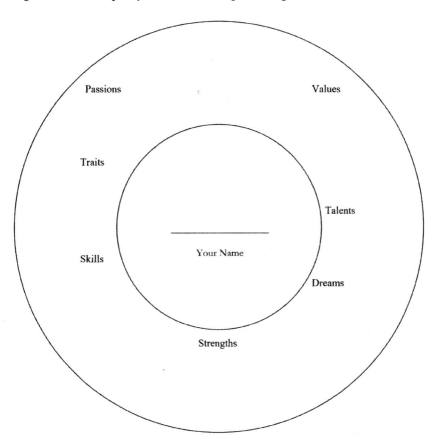

2. Your Seven Circles of Life

Every woman has many personal dimensions, which should lead to numerous life goals. Every woman has different aspects in her life, but sometimes we do not stop to even consider or plan for these different needs and life responsibilities. In today's busy world, prioritizing and fulfilling all of these goals can be downright tough without a systematic approach, a definitive plan. Achieving and living the best life possible becomes more of a challenge if we do not nurture a harmonious balance within these different aspects.

Much like the engine in a car, and the various departments of a corporation, the better all the systems work together, the more efficient and effective is the performance.

To truly begin to live a more contented life, we as women must begin to view ourselves as delicate bionetworks, as ecosystems, or as a soul-system. Just like an ecosystem, all of the components of our lives are interdependent, intimately interrelated. One thing affects another. If one area is grossly neglected, the domino effect comes into play before we realize what has hit us.

Every woman has seven circles of life, seven gardens that she cultivates throughout her life. As you conduct your own personal introspection, finding and achieving a balance that feels right for you is a fundamental task. What are the seven circles of life? Your seven circles are: physical, mental, financial, spiritual, family, career and social.

Now that you know what they are, how do you go about balancing and fulfilling your needs in the seven circles of your life? By setting goals, making a plan, working your plan, by adjusting your plan along the way as needed, and above all, no matter what challenges may come your way, never losing sight of your ultimate goals.

Consider These Possibilities.... When Creating Your Own Seven Circle Goals

accept you, be you, pamper you, relax you, learn about good nutrition, practice prevention, reduce stress, enjoy daily exercise

understanding the balance between mind, body and spirit, developing spiritual resiliency, developing your inner consciousness, understanding and honoring the spiritual laws of nature, developing a religious point of view, connecting with your soul and personal characteristics, discovering your dreams and courageously pursing them

recognizing gifts and talents, recognizing your aptitude, recognizing opportunities for entrepreneurship; understanding job, career, a calling; doing what you love, lifelong learning, purposeful life work

developing interpersonal skills, contributing to community and personal interests, developing friendships and support systems, identifying hobbies and other interests that contribute to your personal development, finding your comfort zone in social settings, nurturing healthy and positive relationships with men and other women

 knowing your inner voices, recognizing invisible chains and buried emotional scars, overcoming an attitude of failure, learning to forgive, your beliefs, being optimistic, choosing to be happy, maintaining a positive mental health

 relationship with your mate, relationships with your parents, communication issues, family skeletons, relationship with children, family chaos, building health family interactions

 budgeting, financial planning, building and maintaining your credit, saving money, retirement income, debt reduction, defining your financial goals, managing your money, investing, and wealth-building

Exercise Four

My Seven Circles of Life Goal Plan

Goal	Sub-goals	Identified Resources Needed to Accomplish Your Goals	Timeline
Physical			
Mental			
Financial			
Family			
Social			
Career			
Spiritual			

Your goals should be challenging, yet reachable. Your goals should be specific, and your goals should include a timeframe for completion.

3. Check Your Attitude

Attitude is everything, and if you do not believe me, watch how differently three women may react to the same situation. One woman may feel devastated by an event, while another is mildly concerned, and yet the other may find the whole situation an interesting challenge that can only serve to help her grow. These totally different viewpoints about the exact same scenario illustrate the difference between women who have a large degree of serenity in their lives and women who do not. One of the biggest differences between people is their attitude and a woman's attitude can propel her to greatness or sink her into a sea of self-destruction. All of our feelings and beliefs are based upon our conscious and unconscious internal thoughts. Your present attitude, whether good or bad is a habit, a habit that you shaped based upon feedback from parents and friends, from the impact that societal factors have had on your perceptions of reality, and from the viewpoints that you have created all by yourself. Combined, all of this goes to form our self-image and our world-image.

Whatever your attitude, your attitude is maintained by the inner conversations that you constantly have with yourself. One of the first steps to changing a negative attitude is to change the inner conversations that swirl around in your head. We are in total control of our attitude whether we realize it or not. From the instant you wake, you can decide to enjoy the beauty of the day or you can choose to step aboard an emotional roller coaster that causes your mood to shift based upon the circumstances of the moment. In the final analysis, we are as happy as we choose to be, plain and simple. Having a positive attitude is a precious attribute that can contribute significantly to the amount of joy you experience in your life. It is up to each of us to decide if we are going to view the teacup half-full or half empty. Each of us have and make choices on a daily basis, and developing an optimistic and upbeat mindset is just one of the decisions we must make. Walking around with a negative attitude, always expecting the worse, filling yourself with pessimism, distrust, fear, anger and fault finding is a heavy burden to carry. You tend to become what you think about, and you feel what you choose. If you find yourself constantly being negative, take the time to find out why.

Understanding that each of our attitudes has three parts can perhaps help to minimize the negativity. One aspect of an attitude is what you know, think or believe about the person or situation, and this is not necessarily based in fact. Regardless, this is the mental element of attitude. Next, there are the feelings that you have about the situation or person. This is the emotional aspect of an attitude. Finally, there are your actions with the person or in the situation. This is the behavioral part of an attitude. Combined, these three form our attitudes, and sadly often the attitude we display is not of our own design.

Often, the attitudes that we walk around with come from a parent, a brother or sister, one bad personal encounter, details we have collected from another person's bad encounter, or from something that we heard. While the mental aspects of our attitudes are generally very complex, the emotional part of an attitude is the most influential and tends to govern how we behave. Working to develop a positive outlook will help you to accomplish your goals for the seven circles of your life. Deciding to choose hope, faith, optimism, enthusiasm, and happiness enables you to face and overcome temporary setbacks and obstacles with vigor. Choosing to be positive can minimize your stress, and enables you to better release your creativity because you are not hindered by the constant fear of failing. So, whether you already have a positive attitude or must admit that your attitude needs a little adjustment, begin to practice the three C's: commitment, control and challenge.

*Commitment—start by making a commitment to yourself to be positive; learn to enjoy your family, friends, and your work; learn to be grateful for all that you have and allow your dreams of success to encourage you to expect more. Give yourself and others praise; earnestly commit to choosing happiness on a daily basis, and if you catch yourself slipping into negativity, take a few moments and determine what factors in the situation are causing you concern.

*Control—work to focus your mind on the positive aspects of every situation, set goals and priorities for the things that you think and do, develop strategies for dealing with difficult situations and practice your actions; learn to relax, be honest with yourself and truly enjoy your successes.

*Challenge—always simply strive to do your best and move on, work to change and improve each day, embrace new opportunities and be open to your infinite possibilities; accept the challenge to know and accept yourself completely. Mastering the 3C's will make you a winner in good times and a thrivor in hard times. Attitude is everything and it is entirely up to you.

Exercise Five   Assessing Your Positive Attitudes

Most often, things that happen to us are beyond our control. However, the way we choose to react to those things is certainly within our power. Our life experiences are a mix of good things and those things that we wish had never occurred. Some people remain positive in spite of challenging times, while some people are miserable, even when good things happen to them. Answer the following 30 items and assess the state of your attitude and your sense of well-being.

For each question circle either: 1-Never, 2-Occasionally, 3-Usually, 4-Often, or 5-Always. Please be honest and candid as you respond to each statement.

My internal thoughts consist primarily of words that are positive, encouraging, and helpful.
1 2 3 4 5

My circle of friends includes only positive minded people with similar interests.
1 2 3 4 5

I acknowledge my strengths, my abilities, all aspect of my personality, and my personal self-worth.
1 2 3 4 5

If I believe I can or cannot do something, I am right.
1 2 3 4 5

I always make a distinction between the things I can and cannot do, and I do not worry about the things that I cannot do anything about.
1 2 3 4 5

I concentrate my energies on finding solutions to an issue rather than focusing on the problems and obstacles.
1 2 3 4 5

I give compliments and demonstrate my appreciation to others and I always avoid criticizing others.
1 2 3 4 5

I always try to make the first thing I say to others something good.
1 2 3 4 5

I take positive steps to eliminate worry about problems that I do have some control over and things that I cannot change for the better.
1 2 3 4 5

I rest and exercise regularly in order to maintain a positive attitude, my energy and personal performance.
1 2 3 4 5

I always try to walk briskly, sit properly, stay relaxed and breathe deeply.
1 2 3 4 5

I practice positive body language to uplift myself, and I always smile.
1 2 3 4 5

I have complied a list of all the positive things I have done in my life, and the action steps I took to achieve them.
1 2 3 4 5

While some stress is inevitable, I know that depending upon my attitude, I can view stress as positive or negative; how I handle stress is up to me.
1 2 3 4 5

I accept that life is filled with both good and challenging days, and I adapt.
1 2 3 4 5

I always look for and expect the best in people realizing that occasionally even if I am disappointed, we both still benefit.
1 2 3 4 5

While someone can stop my progress temporarily, the only person who can stop me permanently is me.
1 2 3 4 5

I do not let red tape or excessive paperwork dampen my spirits when pursuing a goal.
1 2 3 4 5

I try not to blame others because by doing so I am getting farther away from improving things for myself.
1 2 3 4 5

I know that in the end I will lose more by trying to avoid taking risks at all cost.
1 2 3 4 5

I understand that riches usually come not from focusing on obtaining riches, but rather from doing something that I like well.
1 2 3 4 5

I know that a fear of losing something is one sure way to eventually lose it.
1 2 3 4 5

I expect and believe that good things should, can, and will happen to me.
1 2 3 4 5

I do not see difficulties in every opportunity, but opportunities in every difficulty.
1 2 3 4 5

I realize that to make no decision is often a really bad decision.
1 2 3 4 5

I set small goals that I am 95% certain of achieving and as I reach these goals, I set new and larger ones.
1 2 3 4 5

I always try to be well dressed and groomed because it also helps me to feel good.
1 2 3 4 5

I always strive to speak the truth. If I am inclined to lie, I keep silent.
1 2 3 4 5

I know that a large portion of my joy should come from enjoying the work, not just reaching the ultimate goal.
1 2 3 4 5

Learning new things and exploring new challenges is important no matter what a person's age might be, and I look forward to learning something new every day.
1 2 3 4 5

Scoring:
Add up your total score and check out your points against the rankings below:

80-100	Excellent Attitude
60-79	Good Attitude
40-59	Average Attitude
20-39	Below Average Attitude
0-19	Poor Attitude—Seek Help

If you are not pleased with your attitude and would like it to be better, work on improving all 30 items. When you feel that you are consistently doing better, re-take the questionnaire. If you can raise your average by 20 points or more, you are far more positive than before. Remember, these are skill areas that take practice to become automatic. When they do, you will be seeing the fruits of your positive attitude in better results, feelings, more accomplishments in your life and career.

4. The Three Realizations of Life

I ran from them for so long, it was difficult for me to accept them, but in the end I had to acknowledge them, ultimately accepting them as truths. As you work to discover just who you are, understanding your attitudes and beliefs relative to the three realizations is a must.

The three realizations are not some mind boggling, abstract philosophical theories that must be dissected, analyzed and verified before understanding and applying them. The three realizations are simply very basic, extremely realistic positive perspectives that should shape who you are.

> Realization #1 is that your life is your own personal garden, your artistic masterpiece, a tapestry of your own design. Your life can become whatever you choose for it to be, and your life will surely be a reflection of the choices that you make. You are given one precious life to live, to enjoy, to fully participate in, to experience. You control the possibilities for your life, and the sooner you realize this, the easier it becomes to accomplish your life dreams and find personal happiness.

> It does not matter about the circumstances leading to your birth. Whether you lived with both of your parents or only one, the side of town where your lived or if you grew up in poverty, none of that really matters and none of that can stop you from becoming who and what you want to become. Don't worry about who left you or who did you wrong, embrace all of your life experiences as they can help you to learn and grow; embrace them as your experiences can serve as important life lessons that become building blocks for all of your future aspirations. You can create a life of your own design but that is all up to you.

> Realization #2 is that you have to actively, consciously choose. You have to be proactive; you have to decide about the events of your life, and you cannot simply sit back and just allow life to happen to you. Realizing that every action, even inaction creates a result, is a fact that every woman must grow to understand. By becoming a woman of action, a woman learns her strengths, and soon becomes a good decision-maker. A woman must learn the power of decision-making, and she must understand the potency and implications of her choices.

> Through these life lessons, a woman chooses the direction of her life instead of being swept away by circumstances or choices that someone else makes for

her. Taking control of your life minimizes the chances of you ever playing the role of the helpless victim. Some women to get what they want use learned helplessness to manipulate situations. Some women minimize their capabilities and pretend to be less competent than they really are to please others, or as a way to avoid taking action. Decide what you want and act upon it.

While every woman enjoys the beauty of a sunny day, a woman also knows that on occasion the rain will fall. A woman in tune with her spirit understands that life's highway is sometimes filled with bumps and turns.

Realization #3 is that our lives have seasons and nothing, even our challenges lasts forever Navigating this roadway becomes simple once a woman realizes that all things last for only a season.

Knowing this, even when a woman hits a bump in the road, or experiences a setback, she knows that the situation is only temporary. She does not allow herself to become stuck in negativity; paralyzed by the events of one moment in time.

A woman, who has decided to dance through life instead of sleepwalk through it in a daze, refuses to get stuck on life's highway unable to move forward. A woman in touch with herself does not become a bag lady; a woman laden with regrets. In fact, a woman who understands "the realizations" refuses to become burdened down with misguided beliefs, negative thoughts, or remnants left over from past hurts and mistakes. These women are fierce about pursuing their dreams, and they refuse to be denied.

The roadway to personal success and soulful living is not always a straight path. In fact, every woman must journey on her own path, a pathway that unlocks the gateway to her dreams. This path may include a curve called Failure, or a loop in the road called Confusion. She may confront speed bumps called Friends or red lights called Enemies. Maybe even a caution light or two called Family. A woman may face some flats on her path called Jobs. None of this can stop her; none of this will really matter if she has a spare tire called Determination, an engine called Perseverance, and priceless life insurance called Faith.

Allow the three realizations of life to shape the person that you are. Use them to guide the choices that you make. Remember, you only get one life, so treasure it. Put on your favorite dress and shoes, and most definitely enjoy the ride. Always remember, the best is yet to come, you merely have to realize this each day.

I will apply the three realizations to my life as follows:

Exercise 6   REAL WOMEN

Take a moment and think about your definition of REAL WOMEN.
When I think of REAL WOMEN, what comes to my mind is someone who is
Resilient, Earnest, Aware, Limitless,
Wishful, Openhearted, Multifaceted, Expectant and Natural.

What is your definition of a REAL WOMAN, and is that REAL WOMAN you?

THINK ABOUT

- Things that move you to tears
- A most gratifying moment
- Activities you really enjoy doing
- Things you get enthusiastic about
- Things you just do for fun
- Activities you get involved in which cause you to lose track of time
- Activities that make you feel both exhilarated and empowered
- Your personal, social and spiritual values
- Who you admire and why
- Your definition of a ideal life
- Your daydreams
- Your expectations for yourself
- Things that you want to be important in your life
- Your idea of a perfect day
- Hidden personal aspects that you want to develop

A REAL WOMAN…
A REAL WOMAN…
A REAL WOMAN…
A REAL WOMAN…
A REAL WOMAN…
A REAL WOMAN…
A REAL WOMAN…

5. Sister, What Cha Gonna B?

My dear sister, you have got to play the game to win. You are the only one who can decide if you're gonna suit up for the game and what position you're going to play. There are six typical roles that women play, and at different points in time, a woman will find herself playing one of these six. With keen self-awareness, a woman develops a strong ability to spot self-sabotaging behaviors and take action to get herself in check. Every woman has an unique opportunity to decide what her personal mindset is going to be. What are the six roles? The six role types are wishers, waiters, wanderers, wonderers, watchers and players. Sister, my dear sister, what cha gonna b?

Wishers are women who are filled with dreams, and they are always pondering how differently they would like things to be. These women wish that they could get into the game of life, but somehow they never really try. Their hearts are filled with numerous desires, and these women can be found wishing upon a star.

Women who are waiters have dreams too, but they somehow have gotten the misguided notion that a man, a friend or some mystical event is going to jumpstart their lives; so they wait, generally impatiently for something to happen. These women are waiting for someone or something to help them get into the game of life.

Wanderers find it difficult to focus on any one thing. So like a flitting butterfly, this type of woman goes from pillar to post drifting. These women head to the arenas where the game of life is being played, but they get distracted by things all along the way, never making it to any final destination. These women just wander and wander some more, never quite finding themselves, ever.

Wonderers don't have a clue what they want to do with their lives, and these women spend a considerable amount of time trying to figure out what is going on. These women make it to the arena where the game of life is being played, but never make it inside. Women who wonder spend most of their lives questioning, speculating, considering and pondering what they want to be, what they want to do, but sadly it never gets beyond a state of wonderment. It never moves to a state of doing, achieving or moving beyond the question. Before they know what has happened, time has passed, and these women wonder what happened to them and their dreams.

Watchers actually make into the arena where life games are being played. These women take a seat in the stands and that's it. Watchers sit in the stands, see others playing the game and desperately want to participate, but something holds these women back. Something keeps them from living the life of their dreams, pursuing the goals in their heart. Women who watch know that they can play the game as well if not better than the women who are doing things, but for some reason, watchers just can't seem to get started.

Women who are players are in the game of life to win it. Women who are players have specific goals and are willing to give their all working to accomplish them. Women who are players stare fear, disappointment, discouragement and failure squarely in the face and press on regardless.

At different points in my life, I have played all of these six roles, but finally I grew weary of just wishing or wondering; and over time, my spirit kept beckoning me to try, encouraged me to pursue the callings that I carried around in my heart. Making changes and leaving one's comfort zone is difficult, but it can be done.

My fear of leaving this world never trying to do some of the things I really wanted to accomplish eventually outweighed my fear of failing. My fear of taking the gifts I have been blessed with, and the music in my heart to my final resting place has created a sense of urgency in my total being. This has propelled me. Even though my road has been rocky, I have not regretted my decision to live more authentically. I have become spiritually reinvigorated through the pursuit of my dreams. You can too!!!

So, to sisters all around the globe, I say, choose to strut your stuff, choose to sincerely strive to become who you were destined to be. Sister, sister you can "b" what you "c".

Understanding the Roles That You Play

My Roles	Actions I Can Take To Change
When I am/feel _____, I act like a wisher and my behavior is	
When I am/feel _____, I act like a waiter and my behavior is	
When I am/feel _____, I act like a wanderer and my behavior is	
When I am/feel _____, I act like a wonderer and my behavior is	
When I am/feel _____, I act like a watcher and my behavior is	
When I am/feel _____, I do not act like a player and my behavior is	

Fill in the blanks by circling the word (*am or feel*) that best applies to you. Complete the sentence with word (s) that describe your feelings or behaviors when you exhibit these various roles. List ways you can change your attitude and actions so that you do not impede your own progress.

6. The Gifts of Self

A woman's foundation for achieving work and life success, inner and outer peace comes from the gifts of self: self-acceptance, self-love, self-discipline, self-esteem, self-confidence, self-motivation, self-respect, self-love, self-care, self-growth and self-worth.

At the core of the beliefs about ourselves is a woman's response to the statement I AM............

What you are, and what you can become have little to do with your zip code, the kind of neighborhood you grew up in, whether you were raised by only one parent, whether you grew up poor, whether you were physically or mentally abused growing up, whether the other girls at school bullied you, and the list can go on and on and on. Granted, any of these experiences can present a woman with a challenge and definitely may be a source of painful memories. However, once a woman grows to the realization that she does not have to allow any of these situations to limit her, particularly if she honors herself and her life with the gifts of self, she becomes boundless.

Learning to enjoy your own company, learning to love yourself including your body, learning to acknowledge the things you want to change about yourself and your life all come from the gifts of self. The gifts of self unlock your ability to move forward no matter what the circumstances.

It can be difficult for a woman to truly love and accept herself because we tell ourselves, "I'm not slim enough, pretty enough, smart enough, rich enough" or what other personal roadblocks we as women have chosen to claim.

A woman's journey to soulful living must begin by opening the gifts of self one by one, and by learning to appreciate all the treasures found inside.

Self-esteem is a learned behavior, so make it a point to nurture yours on a daily basis. The greatest gift that you can give to yourself is learning to love the skin you're in and learning to appreciate yourself. Far too many women are filled with self-loathing; far too many women dislike everything about themselves, yet they look outside of themselves to others for love, validation, and to confirm their worth as a person. Every woman has things she would like to improve about herself, and that is fine because life-long self-growth is important. Even so, a woman must learn to love herself while on this road to personal improvement. A woman must learn to appreciate the first gift she ever received, the gift of life. To have any chance of joyful living, a woman has got to learn how to like herself. After all, the gift of self is the greatest gift of all.

Exercise 7   My Self-Esteem

Write a history of your self-esteem capturing how you've generally felt about yourself. Use this self-esteem exploration to identify those times when you doubted yourself, as well as actions you took to offer yourself personal encouragement.

Use this activity to further strengthen your self-esteem in the future, and as a tool to help you uncover the real reasons you doubt and discourage yourself. Where did it come from? Who said it? What did they say? Why do you believe it? These are the questions you must ask yourself and honestly answer.

Questions to think about might include................................

- ❑ How do I show love for myself?
- ❑ How do I demonstrate that I know and accept myself?
- ❑ What attitudes and beliefs do I have that strengthen my self-esteem?
- ❑ What attitudes and beliefs do I have that weaken my self-esteem?
- ❑ How do I nurture myself?
- ❑ How worthwhile do I consider myself to be in comparison to others?
- ❑ How do I encourage myself?
- ❑ How do I demonstrate self-respect?
- ❑ How do I display my self-confidence?
- ❑ What are my fears?
- ❑ What are my strengths and opportunities for improvement?
- ❑ What do friends and family say are my strengths and opportunities for improvement?
- ❑ What opportunities for improvement do I accept?
- ❑ How do I heal myself from the past and move on?
- ❑ How do I allow my authentic self to shine through?

7. Become Spiritually Aware

The laws of the universe work 100% of the time, and a life going well is a sign that your thoughts and actions are aligned and are harmonious with these spiritual principles. Granted, life challenges will still come your way, but by being spiritually aware, you will be better able to handle these events. When we find ourselves challenged, sad or plagued by despair, we have somehow violated one of the laws of the universe or we have refused to learn and accept the life lesson that our experiences have sought to teach us. To grow and develop into the woman you want to be, weave the laws of the universe into the tapestry of your very being, into the core of your very soul.

- ✓ The Law of Balance—finding a state of inner balance leads to personal peace; finding mind, spirit and emotional balance; do not allow your habits or the events of your life to move you from your center

- ✓ The Law of Choice—we can not control all of our circumstances but we can choose how we respond to them; feeling in control of our choices makes us feel able to fully create the life that we desire

- ✓ The Law of Process—everything in our lives is a process, step by step, one action after another; pursue everything in your life as a process; an informative journey that nourishes your potential and lends to the accomplishment of your goals

- ✓ The Law of Presence—learn to live with consciousness not reckless abandonment; live in the moment for that is all that you have for sure; learn from the past but do not cling to it; make plans for your future, but first and foremost be present

- ✓ The Law of Compassion—know that one's actions are based upon a person's current beliefs and capacities; understand that those actions are the best that you or the other person can do at that particular moment in time; show compassion and teach it

- ✓ The Law of Faith—understanding that wisdom comes not only from what a woman studies, reads, hears or is told, faith is trusting the wisdom that comes from our spirits, our intuition, the messages that come from our senses; faith is knowing that goodness will always prevail

- ✓ The Law of Integrity—when we live and act in harmony with the spiritual laws of the universe and our own personal visions and value systems, we demonstrate our integrity; we also demonstrate our integrity by inspiring others through our actions

- ✓ The Law of Action—a woman's feelings, knowledge, gifts and talents only come to light through her actions; actions give way to understanding and these new realizations lead to ongoing personal growth

- ✓ The Law of Cycles—just as nature is comprised of cycles, patterns, rhythms and seasons so are our lives; the rotation of the earth, the shifting of the stars, everything happens in its time, everything constantly changes, understand that as cycles come and go, so do the circumstances and situations of our lives

- ✓ The Law of Unity—we are born as separate beings, but just as a raindrop falls and becomes a part of the vast sea, all of us are a part of the family of humanity and we are all affected by similar things in similar ways; realize that a woman should carry a sense of unity in her heart for other women; after all no woman is an island

- ✓ The Law of Surrender—accepting your body, your life, your calling, your place in this moment of time means refusing to block your progress, accepting the will of the higher power; acknowledging your dreams; surrender enables us to use each challenge as an opportunity for personal growth

Exercise 8   A Letter to Me

Write a letter to yourself about yourself.

In this letter detail all of your attributes, and also include those areas of your life that you want to change. Discuss why you want to make these personal changes, and explain how these changes will help you achieve your life goals and dreams. Think about how you will become more personally and spiritually aware.

Imagine that this letter arrives on a day when you are full of self-doubt. What do you say to encourage yourself? Seal the letter and open it in 3 months; see if you have progressed; find out if you have achieved a greater level of personal understanding as you strive to live a more fulfilling life.

Pearls of Wisdom for Soulful Living—Introspection

> A woman who knows, understands and encourages herself is unstoppable.
>
> The self-discovery that a woman finds through introspection can be a reward unto itself for through this process a woman can define her strengths, her dreams, her opportunities for growth, and her heartfelt goals.
>
> A woman who understands the power of introspection looks within, she delves on the inside for answers not on the outside.
>
> Know who you are in order to become who you were meant to be.
>
> A woman who knows understands that money does not equal success, money can not make you feel free,
> money can not make you powerful, money can not make you happy, money cannot be your only goal, and money is not what makes the world go round. A woman who knows understands that money is a tool that opens doors for herself and others.

Vision

THE SECOND KEY TO SOULFUL LIVING

It's amazing to me how the sky at dusk and the sky at dawn looks exactly the same.

At 6:30 in the morning, I crept out of bed, careful not to awaken my husband who slept soundly next to me on his side of the bed. I tipped-toed my way about the room careful not to make any sudden loud noise. Dressed in white sweatpants, a pink sweatshirt and a pair of worn out sneakers, I headed out the door. We were staying in one of the many hotels that dotted the shores of Myrtle Beach in South Carolina. It was one of our getaway weekend trips. When in need of rejuvenation, we always head to the sea.

Outside, the October morning wind blew cool and strong. I love walking on the beach just before the breaking of the day. It's one of those things I can say I really love to do. It makes me feel close to nature. It quiets my mind, it soothes my soul, it enlightens my spirit, it refreshes. If this is not one of the treats you've allowed yourself, try it, and then you will understand what I am saying.

The great teachers of our time rose before sunrise to spend time with their thoughts. They understood that as the night gives way to the morn, our thoughts are most clear.

Slowly, with head bowed, I strolled staring at the zillion grains of sand beneath my feet. I was deep in thought, I felt calm. Now and then I braced myself against a strong gust of wind and I avoided the sudden rush of the waves as the cool water swirled around my feet. A walk on the beach is always therapeutic, a special time for contemplation.

As I walked, I spoke softly to myself. Although calm, I really was not feeling free. There were many questions churning in my mind, but I had no answers. I wondered where my life was going. Where was I taking it? Where should I want to take it? I pondered what I had done and what I should be doing? The power of unanswered questions makes you feel that way, especially when you ask yourself in-depth, provoking and perhaps life-changing questions. On and on I questioned myself, so much so that I could feel my spirit crying out to be heard.

At that moment, my thoughts were numerous and the sun was peeping from behind the ocean. I looked as far as my eyes could see, and I gazed out to where the sky and sea meshed. The sun had risen now and right there before my eyes spread across the sky was the most spectacular display of colors…gold, yellow, orange and red. It was a tapestry of colors splashed across the sky. It was at that moment that I felt inspired, and somewhere the word vision crept into my mind.

For the past couple of months, I had been thinking, meditating and wondering about a vision for my life. From this searching, I realized that I really did not have one. Although I had experienced some levels of success and bouts of personal fulfillment, I was not living with intention and that was the ingredient that was sorely missing.

Have you ever asked yourself the question, "How does someone achieve joy in their lives? How do you find true inner peace?"

It came to me that morning walking on that beach. The answer is to awaken your spirit; awaken it by getting in touch with the very essence of your soul. With that done, the opening of your ears to listen to the mutterings of your soul becomes easier, especially if you allow this soul map to direct your steps. What does this mean? How many times have you asked yourself, "Why am I so discontented? What is my purpose in life? How will I be living five, ten or fifteen years from now? Am I at a dead end or dead lock in my life? What career should I choose? What job is meant for me? Why do I feel so unhappy? Why do I feel as though life has no meaning?"

If you have pondered any of these questions, you are not alone. These were the questions that raced through my head as I listened intently to the sound of the surf. I found my answer to these questions as I uncovered and gained a better understanding of having vision.

What is vision? How will you find it? What will vision do for you?

Vision is your inner eye to see and to find what your spirit is looking for from within. Deep inside of you in your soul, in your spirit, lies an unexpected and undiscovered love. What do your truly and sincerely love? Have you forgotten what it is that you love? Your dreams and the hopes that lie in some undiscovered place within you long to come out, long to be realized.

How will you find your vision? Simply stop, look and listen to the urgings of your soul; dig and uncover your personal diamonds; there in that place you will find your vision, your calling and your personal passions; there you will find the lifework that you were meant to do.

Vision is crucial, for vision will affect how you live your life and the person you choose to become. Far too many of us have no vision for our lives or we've lost sight of it. Sadly, you may discover that you are not the person that you set out to become or the person that your true spirit calls you to be. It could be that without a vision you have lost your way. Becoming your true self is the easiest and hardest thing for a woman to do.

What have you lost? What do you want? What makes you happy? What gives you joy? Deep down you know what you are looking for, and the question becomes do you have the courage to pursue it persistently. You know why you feel restless and unfulfilled. If you've been trying to find your way, look within. You can choose to answer the calling of your soul by creating a vision for you life.

On that breezy day while walking by the sea, I found my vision. I found direction and meaning for my life. Decide to have a vision for your life and believe completely in your vision. Through your vision you will find your way to a state of soulful living.

Who are women with vision?

A woman with vision can see opportunity in an obstacle and she has the courage to act upon it. A woman with vision knows exactly the direction she wants her life to take and she has a definite plan to get there.

Vision is the ability to see who you are and the perception to know who you can become; vision is being keenly aware of all of your talents and natural gifts and imagining the countless ways that you can use them to bring joy to yourself but especially to others; vision is charting a course for your life; and vision is choosing to blaze your own trail instead of waiting for someone else to clear the path.

Far too many women waste their lives on anger, bitterness, sadness and regret. These are the fruits of a life without direction, a life without visionary goals. Goals determine your thoughts and your thoughts determine your life. Without goals, a woman fails to tap into the best of herself and in the absence of this she will never accomplish anything of significance. A woman without a vision cannot flourish; she will merely exist. Realize that introspection gives way to vision and vision uncovers the trail to your ultimate destiny.

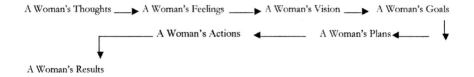

No matter what your circumstances might be, no matter where you are right now, you have the capacity to create a vision for your life. By opening your eyes and getting in tune with your spirit, you can achieve your destiny. Choose to seek you vision; speak your vision; seek your vision and savor your vision. Ask yourself, "What do I truly enjoy? What would I do without being paid? What things come easy to me but seem to be difficult for others? What do others say are my gifts and talents, the things I do well?" Refuse to sleepwalk through your life, and do not allow your life to be nothing more than a collection of situations.

Your vision should be specific and a reflection of your imagination. Your goals and purpose should give your vision its specificity, and the images in your mind and the dreams of your spirit should bring vivaciousness to your vision.

Whether your vision is to work with youth, write books, teach and encourage others, start a community organization, create a business, or transform your community, see your vision clearly in your mind and then use all of your might to achieve it.

Exercise 1   What Do I Want???

List seven things that you envision yourself doing, narrow those seven down to four, to two and then by identifying the primary vision that you have for your life. Remember from your core vision other goals will develop and perhaps expand your original vision. The process of clearly identifying your vision is a critical first step.

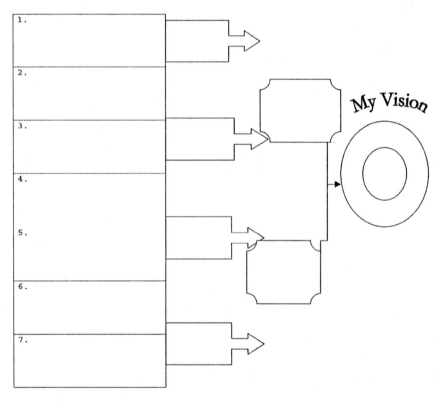

Key Two VisionA Woman's Guide to Soulful Living

1. Hey, Where Are You Going?

One day I was walking down the street and I did not see where I was going. Though I could not see, I kept on walking, and I walked and walked and walked some more. I turned the corner and before I knew it I was on another street. I kept on walking.

The next day I just started walking again. I tripped and fell into a hole and I just kept on walking. I walked and walked and girl I kept on walking. I turned a second corner but I fell into another bigger hole. That did not stop me because I simply kept on walking. The more I walked, the farther away from home I went. But I kept on walking.

One day, I grew weary and I just stopped walking, and I said to myself, "Where are you going?" I replied, "I do not know".

I said to myself, "Where do you want to go?" I said, "I do not know." I asked myself "Why are you in this hole?" And I said, "I don't know." I then asked myself, "Do you want to get out of this hole?" I said to myself, "What hole?"

I kept walking and asking myself these questions over and over until one day I got sick and tired of being sick and tired, so I searched until I understood the questions and was able to find the answers. On that day I got in touch with my spirit and found my vision. Then, I began living.

When a woman is able to answer this question, "Where Are You Going?" with certainty and conviction, she has truly discovered her purpose. This is a woman with a vision for her life. Once a woman understands and accepts herself, finding purpose for her life is the beginning of infinite possibilities. Defining the things that you want to achieve in your life helps a woman to develop a plan and then focus her efforts. Women who achieve their dreams in life are fully guided by personal purpose. It is well worth a woman's time to identify her heart's passion in order to find personal clarity.

To find your purpose, you must uncover your burning desires, those things that by their achievement would fill your life with immeasurable joy. When you think of your passions, think of pass-I-on. When you think about it, your passions should reflect who you are. Every woman wants to help her family and others in her own special way; every woman wants to leave her mark on the world. These are the elements of passion and purpose; your unique purpose; those dreams in your heart that you were put on this earth to do.

The things that you desire to accomplish should reflect the person that you are and the activities that you enjoy. Your calling should be pursuits that incorporate your gifts, talents, values and personality. Whether you think of purpose as bliss, a calling, or meaning, each woman if she is honest with herself has an intense interest to identify and express her life purpose. Finding purpose for your life is an important spiritual journey that serves to help a woman shape the direction of her life. Sister, know where you are headed at all times and stay focused.

Finding your purpose helps you to specialize in the things that compel your attention. This specialization helps you to become highly proficient in your chosen area. Purpose causes you to budget your time and money wisely. Why? Because once you have crafted a vision for your life, and that vision is centered on your purpose, you will spend your energy and your money to make this goal a reality.

Purpose opens your eyes and heart to opportunities that come your way, and your decisions and choices are made with your purpose at the forefront of your thoughts. When you know what your purpose is, you are better able to attract cooperation, and your level of personal faith increases as a result of this focus. Without purpose, a woman is like a lost traveler without a map or someone walking on a sandy beach with their eyes closed tightly. Finding purpose for your life will give meaning and direction to everything that you do. By having a purpose for you life, you will soon enjoy everything that you do because now you have a clear vision for the things that you want to achieve.

Choose your personal window of opportunity.

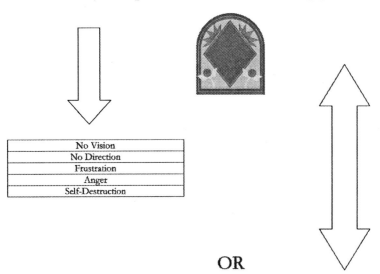

No Vision
No Direction
Frustration
Anger
Self-Destruction

OR

Vision
Destination
Plan
Direction
Effort

Exercise 2   My Purpose Is.........................

Ask yourself the following questions and answer yes or no. Find your purpose by focusing on your talents and your interests, and then go on…go on……go on…go on……………………………………………..………GO!!!!

Part I

Do you enjoy the work that you currently do?
Do you feel excited about going to work most days?
Do you ever feel like your work and leisure time activities are the same?
Do you feel that everything is all right in your personal world?
Do you still enjoy the work that you do, even when you get a little frustrated?
Do you feel that there is absolutely nothing else you'd rather be doing?
Would you say that you are at peace with your life?
Do you possess the trust that things will work out in your life?
Do you have a positive attitude?
Does the work that you do energize you?

My Interests Are............

Part II Do It On Purpose

Complete these sentences, so that you can uncover your passions and define your purpose.

I feel my heart pounding and beating with excitement whenever I
I truly feel good about myself when I
I seem to always lose track of time whenever I
I get emotional when I
If I could be any person in history, I would be
If I was locked in a library, I would spend most of my time reading about
If I had to describe what I feel called to do, it would be to do
If I could only accomplish one thing in my life, it would be to
If I could create one thing, it would be
If I had to list two thing I am good at, it would be
I dream about my future and I see myself
I would work as a professional in the career field of_____even without pay because I simply enjoy it

Find Your Purpose

My Divine Purpose In Life Is To	I See Myself Doing _____ For Other	I Want To Serve_____	I Want to Achieve My Goal of _____
Anita Davis-DeFoe's Purpose In Life Is To……	Educate, Inspire and Encourage	Women and Girls Everywhere	Teaching them to use their talents to develop all aspects of their potential.
1.			
2.			
3.			
4.			
5.			
6.			
7.			

Seven Things I Want To Accomplish In My Life

2. You Better Recognize

Whether its motivating others, organizing events, operating a business, teaching, singing, mentoring, acting, helping others, cooking, home decorating, entertaining, painting, speech making, whatever it may be, recognizing your gifts and talents is one of the most exciting discoveries you can make. Discovering your gifts and talents can also be one of the most difficult tasks a woman can ever undertake.

A woman who is aware of her personal gifts is better able to figure out what she wants to do with her life. The average woman will work between 750,000 and 1,000,000 hours before retiring. So, certainly finding a work and leisure activity that you truly enjoy makes these numbers less daunting. Ideally, your day job should use all of your talents and provide you with a tremendous amount of fulfillment. There are countless women who have found jobs or projects that they enjoy so much that their daily activities do not even feel like work. This is because they truly enjoy what they are doing.

Too often, this is not the case. Unfortunately, for most women, their jobs are simply a way to make money to pay for daily needs. This situation is generally not the case when a woman has taken the time to discover her personal strengths and deepest dreams. Maybe your job is only a piece of a larger puzzle as you pursue your divine purpose. Maybe you need to change your vocation and start working in another field altogether, or maybe your job meets a financial need for now, while your need to fulfill your purpose, your calling is met through other avenues.

Typically, if you revisit your childhood dreams, there you will find your purpose. Try to remember those things that you immersed yourself in; try to remember what you were doing when you became upset that you had to stop and go to bed or do your chores. Most often, this will provide snapshots of your natural gifts, and therein lays your clues to your life purpose. Were you writing poetry, sewing an outfit that you designed yourself, or composing a tune on the steel pan? Were you writing short stories, playing the piano, or pretending to be a teacher, lawyer, doctor or nurse? Were you planting a garden, or caring for a variety of pets?

Try to remember your heartfelt dreams before they became contaminated by fear and self-doubt, beaten down by opinion. Try to discover your natural talents and your consistent interests. Determine those interests that compel you to dream, to create, to aspire to something more. These are the things that will lead you to your life's purpose and calling.

If you do not have a motivating purpose or heartfelt dreams at the moment, you are not alone. Most women are just going with the flow, but sooner or later, a woman will want and need more.

Find a dream that inspires you, consumes your thoughts and ignites you to chase it.

Decide to accept personal responsibility for creating the life that you desire, decide to use your divine talents to accomplish your dreams and to give your life purpose. Doing something that you enjoy will no doubt add another dimension to your life, and the joy that you experience from this discovery will be beyond your greatest expectations.

My Childhood Dreams Were To:
1.
2.
3.
4.
5.
6.
7.

The Passion Circle

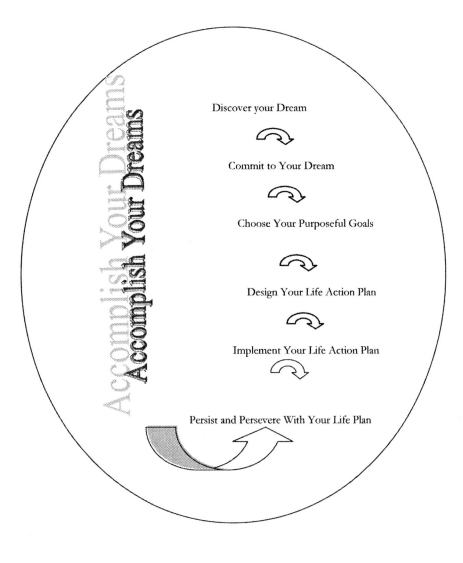

Exercise 3   My Life Plan

Create a plan for your life. Make a plan and put it into action. If you do not have a plan for your life, someone else surely does. List your gifts and talents. Think of the kind of activities and projects that you enjoy. Determine how you want to use your talents and think about the roles you want to play working in the areas that excite you. Are you a teacher, encourager, motivator, supporter, listener, peacemaker, or mentor? What roles will you play and how will you use these roles to accomplish your purpose? Dream and set goals that relate to your personal purpose. Remember the achievement of your purpose may be on the job or it may be through a business or project that you create. Do not confuse a job with your calling. Ideally, they should be one in the same, but if not, do not despair. Just remain focused on the purpose in your heart and opportunities will present themselves to you. Every woman is divinely created to contribute something to better the world, choosing to do so is another story. Begin to do everything on purpose. Start listening to your spirit and follow your heart.

My Life Plan

My Gifts and Talents:

Activities I Enjoy:

My Life Mission, My Purpose:

Affirmations That I Use to Encourage Myself to Pursue My Personal Purpose:

My Life Role Is:

My Dream In This Role Is:

My Short Term Goal In This Role Is:

My Long Term Goal In This Role Is:

3. Ponder Phenomenal Potential

Maybe you are deeply religious, or maybe you are still getting your religious life together. Perhaps you are very spiritual, and then again maybe you are still trying to connect the dots between your spirit, your soul and your life. Whatever the case may be, I ask you to consider reading the Parable of the Talents found in the Holy Bible; Matthew 25:14-30. This parable is much more than just a biblical teaching; the message that this parable gives us is an important life lesson.

A parable is a simple story that is true to life; a story that compares two unlike things to teach us an important spiritual truth. The Parable of the Talents is the story of three servants who are each given "talents," which in biblical times referred to money. Each servant was charged to nurture and to be the custodian over his talents in the master's absence. Two of the servants invested their time and energies wisely and from these seeds expanded the talents into more. While one servant out of laziness, fear and self-doubt dug a hole in the ground and buried his talent in order to keep it safe. While the two who had worked hard were rewarded with more talents, the servant who did not use the talent that he had been given lost it.

When this parable is related in religious settings or motivational speeches, the message is always that each of us has a tremendous amount of potential, but so few of us choose to honor it. Your potential is that shining star that burns inside your heart and your spirit; a shining star that wants to be revealed, be projected. Your shining star waits patiently for you to introduce it to the world so that it can reflect and fully manifest your potential.

Potential is a treasure hidden inside of you, much like the journey of a newborn going from a cell to a human spirit. Potential must be nurtured and tended so that it can eventually flourish. Potential is the jewels concealed in your spirit and through your spirit, a vision for your life is revealed to you. From this vision you uncover a purpose for your life, and you then set goals to claim it. That is if you choose to determine your genuine lifework, and if you choose to answer the call of your true spirit. Potential is also the numerous qualities that you possess that make you who you are; potential forms the foundation for who you can become. My definition of potential is simply:

*P*ersonal
*O*pportunities
*T*o
*E*ffectively
*N*urture
*T*alents
*I*ntently
*A*dvantageously
*L*imitlessly

Every woman is uniquely endowed with potential greatness; every woman is born with at least one talent, generally more. Some women recognize and acknowledge their talents choosing to use them to lead a purposeful life in a meaningful way. Others spend years refusing to embrace and use their potential, before finally waking up to realize that they are wasting their lives and missing out on buckets of joy. Sadly, some women never wake up and end up spending their whole lives unfulfilled and constantly depressed.

Potential and talents are precious possessions, and the more you develop your potential and use your talents the more skilled you become. This is the spiritual law of practice at work. When you fail to develop your potential, over time circumstances, choices, and the attitudes that you develop snuff out your bodacious potential. Over time, talents are lost or the quality of the talent is diminished if you do not recognize it, treasure it, use it and safeguard it.

Ponder your potential on a daily basis. Make certain that you are investing your talents wisely and that you are seeking to do good in the world using your talents. To live the most joyful life that you can begins with aspiring to live up to the potential inside of your soul. Seek to develop your potential completely, choose to travel your pathway to personal fulfillment.

Ponder your potential using these two reminders:

$$A \times A + A = A$$
(Attributes), times (Aptitudes), plus (Attitude) equals (Altitude)

Simply put, consider the things that are your natural talents (Attributes), the things that you are good at without much effort (Aptitudes), add a positive attitude to this, and the sky is the limit (Altitude). Your possibilities are limitless if you harness your potential and allow yourself to see where it takes you.

$$IC + AA + PMA + PPP = AWP$$
(Innate Characteristics) plus (Acquired Attributed), plus
(Positive Mental Attitude) plus
(Purpose, Passion and Persistence) equals A Woman's Potential

Take you Innate Characteristics (IC-the strengths you are born with), add your Acquired Attributed (AA—the things you learn to do), add a Positive Mental Attitude (PMA-develop a can do spirit), and then add Purpose, Passion and Persistence (PPP—goals you want to achieve that focus on lifework that you passionately want to do; lifework that you are determined to do), altogether this equals A Woman's Potential (AWP).

Potential is unexposed ability, reserved power, untapped strength, unused success, dormant gifts and hidden talents. Potential is the sum of who you are that is yet to be revealed; it's a deposit that waits to be released and maximized. It's being capable of much more than you presently think.

Potential can be an extremely fleeting commodity. Every woman has it but not every woman decides to act upon it and use it to create the life that she wants. Far too many women walk around with the ability to achieve so much and to be all the things that they desire. If they were to admit it, a great deal of women no longer even think about their potential or how they can use it. The vast majority of women are merely going through the motions of life, while their potential is being allowed to diminish. The longer potential is wasted, the more difficult it becomes to manifest it, or to even use it because new challenges present themselves every day. The longer potential goes untapped, the harder a woman has to work to revive it. It is never too late to accomplish your dream; you just have to want it.

Girl, you definitely got potential, now what are you going to do with it!!

64 • A Woman's Guide to Soulful Living

Exercise 4   The Fruits of Your Success

List your gift and talents on the arrows and write inside the circle how you will use this talent to achieve your purpose.

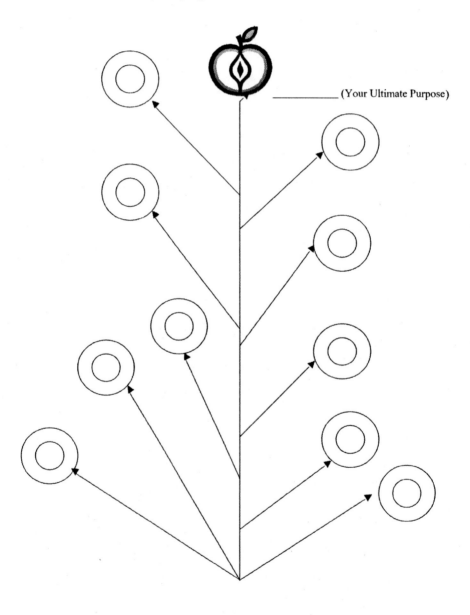

_____ (Your Ultimate Purpose)

4. Go for the Goal

A woman's goals are guideposts as she journeys to her vision. Goals are a woman's own special treasures; goals order a woman's steps. Before you proceed, make certain that you understand the difference between a goal and a wish. A wish goes something like this, "I wish I were wealthy." "I wish I were thin." "I wish I had a better job." A wish is a daydream, a fleeting fantasy spoken at the moment. Wishes are not out of reach, the only problem with wishes are that generally they are not linked to any specific plan of action. Wishes have their place, particularly if they lay the groundwork for more definitive goals, but no woman can spend her entire life just wishing.

A goal is a specific desired outcome that you set for yourself. Your goals are not an end in themselves. Typically, while you are vigorously pursuing your goals, they become stepping-stones to other goals that emerge as you successfully achieve goal after goal on your list, and you should have a list. If you do not have a goal list make one. A woman's ability to achieve her goals increases when they are written. I have always been more prone to pursue and achieve personal goals when I've written them down, and I am certain that this process will also work for you.

Take your visioning process one step further and create goal maps; a goal map can be a visual guide for your vision. Follow these steps to create your own personal goal maps. All you need is paper and pen.

Step 1 *Dream It—What do you want to achieve?*
Visualize your dreams, define your seven circle goals; prepare your goal list

Step 2 *Organize It—Which goal comes first?*
Select your top five goals. Prioritize your goals and determine your number one goal. Your number one goal should contribute to the achievement of your other goals.

Step 3 *Picture It—What does your goal look like?*
Communicate your goal through pictures; simple to complex drawings, even symbols will do.
Put a picture of your number one goal in the center of the paper. Draw a circle around it and draw lines or branches all around it connecting to pictures of your other four goals.

Step 4   *Understand It—Why is this goal important to you?*
Our emotions give our thoughts impact and power; emotions act as fuel for our motivation. Identify your emotional reasons for achieving the goal and place these reasons at the top of the page.

Step 5   *Define It—When do you want to achieve your goal?*
Determine a date to achieve your goal and write it under the goal in the middle of the page; jot down the day's date, and draw two parallel lines connecting the two dates. This is your goal timeline.

Step 6   *Plan It—Which steps will it take to achieve your goals?*
Identify the steps you will need to take to accomplish your goals. Write them on the branches on the right side of the timeline. Place the actions that you can take today on the bottom of the page and take your first steps today.

Step 7   *Implement It—Who are the people that you need to support your efforts to achieve your goals?*
List family, friends and the professionals you will need help from to accomplish your goals. Write their names on the branches on the left side of the timeline, put their names beside the actions you want the person to help you with.

Your Goal Map

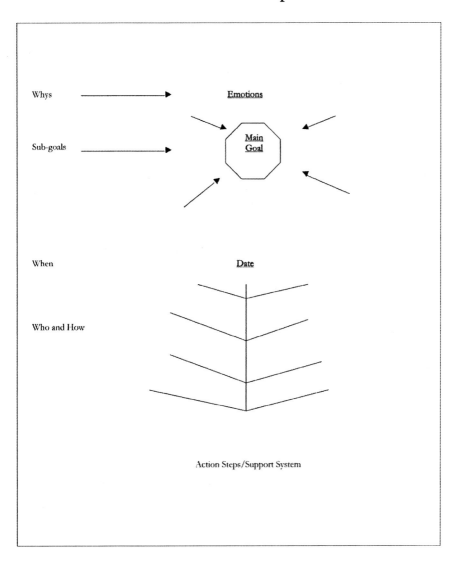

5. A Matter of Choice

Although it should come as no surprise, so much of what we achieve, so many of life's pleasures that we derive, so many things that find a resting place in our lives first begin with our choices. Choice is the act of making a selection from among several options. Choice is deciding upon the most beneficial option. Choice is deciding upon a course of action that accomplishes or moves you closer to your ultimate goal. Choice is not always clear, not always easy to identify, not always easy to make.

When I reflect on my life, I realize now that what I did not fully understand then has led to all the good things that have occurred in my life, as well as all of the things that I would love to have a second chance to change. In retrospect, I now know that a women's ability to make choices enables her to better control the direction her life takes, and helps her to take positive and productive steps toward her vision, her personal goals.

A woman is totally free up to the point of choice, from that point on, the choice controls the chooser; that is until another choice is made. Once coming to grips with the fact that the events of our lives are all a matter of choice, a woman can learn to weigh her choices thoroughly and instead of opting for short-term pleasure, she can choose long-term satisfaction.

Learning to consistently make choices that contribute to your good can be difficult. Women by their very nature seek to please and nurture others. We want people to like us, love us, need us, and sometimes we allow our needs and our nature to override our common sense. Often, we make choices based upon how we think others will react, not necessarily the best choice to fit the situation. Finding a way to balance your choices considering all of the factors that matter to you is an art that can be learned. I have learned that achieving this personal balance is challenging, but possible, and certainly necessary. I have learned, sometimes as a result of intense pain, our choices, not our conditions determine our destiny. I now know that our choices impact our ability to create the life of our dreams. Our choices lead to consequences, sometimes consequences that we have not even considered.

Making choices involves deciding what to focus on, knowing what things are important to you, and determining what actions to take to create the results that you want.

Get comfortable with your choices by speaking them out loud. Fill in the blanks, "I want to_____," (the result you desire). Test your desire by saying, "With all of my heart and from the depths of my soul, I chose to _____." (the commitment to the choice you are about to make)

Learning to choose is liberating. Learning to make heartfelt choices is an important tool for soulful living. Choices give women power, and your choices can serve to define who you are and the life you end up leading.

Remember the big six when you think about making choices. (1) Understand the significance of your choices; (2) Commit to your choices fully and follow through; (3) Make choices frequently and you will become more comfortable making such decisions; (4) Learn from your choices so that your ability to make future decisions improves over time; (5) Alter your choices when situations change; and (6) Learn to enjoy making choices, for matters of choice become the foundation for your life.

In the end your life and state of being reflects the choices you have made, the paths you have chosen to take. Every woman's life can be or become whatever she wants, it is just a matter of choice.

Exercise 5   Check Your Choices

Get in the habit of systematically checking your choices before making a decision. Write down the situation, and the facts that surround the situation. Stick with the facts, not your emotions or someone else's opinion. Think of three choices that you could make; consider the benefits and concerns associated with each possible choice. Review all of this information carefully and then reach a decision that helps you to move closer to or achieve your goal.

The Situation	Details About the Situation	
The Facts	What Are the Facts??	
	Benefits	Concerns
Choice One		
Choice Two		
Choice Three		
Decision		

Choosing **H**eartfelt **O**pportunities **I**ntelligently **C**onsciously **E**veryday

6. No Buts About It

We have all begun some task, some activity, some goal that went unfinished. I can certainly compile a list of such projects that over the years I just sort of left hanging. When I forced myself to come to grips with my failure to complete the project, somehow I have eased my own conscience by allowing the words "but I" to creep into my self-talk.

Self-talk comes in several forms; there is the inner critic, the negative voice we listen to most often; the inner defender, the voice that makes excuses for our bad behavior, and then there is the inner guide, the voice we hear but are reluctant to listen to and are afraid to trust because we know it is right. Reframing your self-talk is a must if you are to sincerely achieve your dreams and bring more joy into your life. The raining downpours of life are plentiful enough, so being your own source of negativity is an impediment that you do not need.

Whenever you find yourself saying, "But I Can't," "But I Don't Have," "But I just wonder if," begin changing your self-talk. Also, ask yourself, "Why am I filling my own head with doubt?" When you find yourself consumed with discomfort, fear, frustration, disappointment or inadequacy, it is time for some serious action; it is time for you to figure out why you are limiting yourself.

Deciding to display dogged persistence can put all of these mental progress stoppers to rest. When you couple passion and personal purpose with persistence, your sustained efforts will help you to achieve your desired results. With persistence, particularly persistence pursuing positive action, there is nothing that you cannot achieve, no obstacles you cannot overcome.

Go forth and pursue your vision, and let there be no ifs, or buts about it.

7. Its At The Door

Too often women give up just as they approach the achievement of their ultimate goal, just when what they seek is at the door. When a woman gives in, it is because she has lost her will to win, she has lost faith in herself. A woman must always remember that without struggle there is no personal growth, and without growth, there can be no victory.

Common obstacles that can hinder your persistence are procrastination, fear of criticism or the fear of failure. Procrastination will cause you to put off till tomorrow something that you need to do today. Procrastination can rob you of your time, and wasting your time is the same thing as wasting your talents.

There are 86,400 seconds in a day and if given that much cash on a daily basis, most women would spend it, and a great deal of that money would be spent wisely. But what happens when it comes to our time, we often fail to invest it as wisely; many women just fritter it away.

Fear of criticism makes us lose our personal drive, diminishes our self-confidence and hampers our inner source of creativity. A woman must learn to hear constructive criticism but refuse to let it define her actions or stifle her progress. This is where being in tune with self and one's personal vision for life comes in handy. This self-awareness gives a woman tremendous confidence in the face of all kinds of criticism, constructive or destructive.

Allowing fear of failure to hamper your progress is because you still have the attitude that one failure is the final curtain to a dream. This kind of attitude fuels the belief that if you experience one failure, you cannot continue to press on, a belief that your dream cannot be achieved. This could not be further from the truth.

Failures are merely stepping-stones to ultimate success. Actually, what we call failure is nothing more than an indicator that the course of action selected needs to be changed. In fact, I prefer to think of failure as *F*inding *A*nswers *I*n *L*ife's *U*nanticipated *R*esistant *E*ffect. Use these steps to get into the habit of being persistent.

(1) Develop a defined, internal vision of your personal purpose, and a passion to realize your dreams.

(2) Take your vision and develop specific goals to achieve your vision. Your goals should serve as your targets and become the focus of your energy and your action.
(3) Create an action plan to accomplish your goals; also map your goals if you find that be helpful. If not, make sure to at least write them down.
(4) Have a master mind alliance of 2-3 people who can serve as your support system and encourage you in your efforts.
(5) Understand that failures are lessons learned and are only temporary setbacks; actually setups to ultimate success.
(6) Comprehend that you do not get something for nothing and through your continued efforts you will prevail.
(7) Take daily actions toward the achievement of your goals and your ultimate dreams.

You must decide to pursue your goals with the tenacity of a pit bull holding tightly to his favorite bone. Hold tight to your dreams my sister and refuse to let go.

To create lasting change, raise the standards for your life, or get rid of the attitudes and beliefs that are holding you back, change your strategy and keep changing it until you find what works for you.

There are seven common roles women play when it comes to pursuing their vision and lifework, and its up to you to decide who you are going to be.

- The Achiever—set her goals and does not give up, EVER
- The Quitter—starts something, but gives up at the first sign of trouble; the quitter rarely finishes anything that she starts
- The Procrastination—tomorrow, tomorrow, I'll get started tomorrow, a woman who procrastinates finds it difficult to start a task; she allows small challenges to become major roadblocks
- The Planner—she is great at making a plan, but working the plan is another story
- The Blamer—she always plays the blame game for not achieving her goals, she feels that someone else is always holding her back
- The Complainer—nothing is ever right and she complains all the time, all this time spent complaining impedes her progress because she doesn't have much time to do anything else
- The Doubter—she has no confidence in her ability to achieve her goals, doubt keeps her from trying and from aspiring

What you aspire to is right at the door. All you have to do is open up the door to opportunity; walk through, and make yourself comfortable.

Pearls of Wisdom for Soulful Living—Vision

> Strive to keep your imagination in focus because without it you will not be able to see.
>
> All that a woman does is linked to how well she can see possibility.
>
> A woman can only receive what she sees herself receiving, and a woman can only grow as much as her horizon allows.
>
> Open your eyes to your potential, your promise, and your possibilities. Fully embrace the song in your heart, and the yearnings of your spirit.

Habits

THE THIRD KEY TO SOULFUL LIVING

Who Am I?
(Anonymous)

I am your constant companion.
I am your greatest helper or heaviest burden. I will push you onward or drag you down to failure.
I am completely at your command.
Half the things I do you might just as well turn over to me and
I will be able to do them quickly and correctly.
I am easily managed-you must merely be firm with me.
Show me exactly how you want something done
and after a few lessons I will do it automatically.
I am the servant of all great individuals and,
Alas, of all failures, as well.

Those who are great, I have made great.
Those who are failures, I have made failures.
I am not a machine, though I work with all the precision of a machine
plus the intelligence of a human. You may run me for a profit
or run me for ruin-it makes no difference to me.
Take me, train me, be firm with me, and I will place the world at your feet. Be easy with me and I will destroy you.

I AM HABIT!!!!

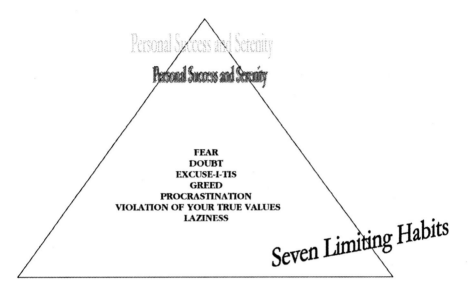

AUTOBIOGRAPHY IN FIVE SHORT CHAPTERS
by
Portia Nelson

I
I walk down the street.
There is a deep hole in the sidewalk
I fall in.
I am lost ...I am helpless.
It isn't my fault.
It takes me forever to find a way out.

II
I walk down the same street.
There is a deep hole in the sidewalk.
I pretend I don't see it.
I fall in again.
I can't believe I am in the same place
but, it isn't my fault.
It still takes a long time to get out.

III
I walk down the same street.
There is a deep hole in the sidewalk.
I see it is there.
I still fall in ...it's a habit.
my eyes are open
I know where I am.
It is my fault.
I get out immediately.

IV
I walk down the same street.
There is a deep hole in the sidewalk.
I walk around it.

V
I walk down another street.

What Street Will You Choose????

Key Three Habits

1. Life Patterns

As I struggle to improve the quality of my life, I constantly reflect on why my life is not quite where I want it to be. I have goals in all seven circles of my life that are yet to be realized. I search hard for causes, external factors, even people that I can somehow hold accountable for my inability to move forward. As I do this personal reflection, common themes, similar situations, even behaviors and choices parallel each other.

Over the last couple of years, more and more I have taken my head out of the clouds. I have forced myself to take a closer look at my life. What I have come to realize is that I have repeated a number of actions over the course of time. My behaviors and choices have remained consistently the same when faced with various situations. Surprisingly, when I analyzed the patterns of my life, I have grown to understand that where I am is exactly because of where I am…mentally and emotionally. I had to acknowledge that the habits I have cultivated, nurtured and safeguarded over the years have led to the challenges I presently face; my current station in life.

Painful as it may be, to achieve desired life changes, a necessary first step is to look at the events of your life and determine how your habits have contributed to where you are in contrast to where you want to be.

Our life patterns reflect our values, our beliefs, our attitudes, our responses to certain situations. In most instances, we have gotten so comfortable with our "personal way of doing business" that we don't even recognize that some of our habits are holding us back. Until you stop and conduct a genuine life check-up, it is not possible to make the necessary and critical life changes needed to move forward. Although sometimes arduous, change is critical so that you can create the life of your dreams, so that you can experience the inner peace that you desire.

Take the time to determine what actions and behaviors have contributed to where you find yourself. Take stock of your personal habits completely. Celebrate and use the habits that contribute positively to your life, and work to let your non-beneficial habits go. Once you understand the past and present patterns of your life; you can re-chart your behaviors and effectively create a new blueprint for your future.

Look at your life patterns closely, though it may be a little agonizing at times, doing so will help to uncover self-defeating behaviors. This knowledge can help you to change your behavior, free yourself from these personal shackles, and ultimately enable you to flourish. Refocus your life patterns because when you do, you change your thinking and your beliefs; when you change your beliefs, you change your expectations; when you change your expectations, you change your attitude; when you change your attitude, you change your behavior; when you change your behavior, you change your performance, and when you change your performance, you change your life!!!

Life Reflections

Common Life Situations You Have Faced	Habits That Have Led To These Reoccurring Situations

Exercise 1

Are You Stuck In the Mud!!!!

WHAT HABITS ARE KEEPING YOU FROM ACHIEVING YOUR GOALS, FEELING
PERSONAL CONTENTMENT?
ACKNOWLEGE THEM, CONFRONT THEM, CONQUER THEM

1._____ 2._____ 3._____

4._____ 5._____ 6._____

My Soulful Living Habits

Habits You Will Develop To Foster Personal
Growth, More Personal Fulfillment and Joy

1.
2.
3.
4.
5.
6.
7.

2. Destiny Habits

One day a conversation with a dear friend revealed her fear that she would spend her entire life unfocused and without direction. My friend was deeply concerned that she would somehow fail to be the person that she was intended to become.

Listening to her earnestly share her feelings, I wondered what I could say to calm her uneasiness, what words I could find to assure her that what she envisioned would certainly not be her fate. Finally, I said through my own life journey I had finally learned that no matter how many goals I set and the countless action plans I create, what I have ultimately been able to achieve in my life has been directly tied to my habits. I told her that once a woman understands that what she gets out of life is not what she hopes for but what she is and what she does, personal and life transformation becomes within her reach. Making all of this possible are our habits, and our habits are the actions that drive our daily behaviors. Our habits pave the way to our future, our destinies. I shared that I struggle to overcome my bad habits daily.

Our habits shape who we are, what we do, the choices we make, the roads we take. Our habits can be positive and contribute fully to our productive development, or our habits can slowly lead us down a trail so negative that we become stymied, eventually finding ourselves in a cycle of personal destruction. Behaviors in as few as seven days become comfortable, find a resting place within us, and before we realize what has happened, the behavior has become a habit. Be careful what behaviors you make your friend because your habits can make or break you. Besides, it takes a minimum of twenty-one days, and in some cases a lifetime to break a bad habit. A close look at a person's past actions can tell you why they are exactly where they are. This quick life scan can often predict what is to be in days to come.

Habits, both mental and actual, to avoid include: poverty, imaginary illness, procrastination, negativity, laziness, envy, greed, vanity, cynicism, purposelessness, irritability, revenge, jealousy, dishonesty, arrogance, sadism, learned helplessness, pettiness and the list goes on. Habits to embrace include: definiteness of purpose, faith, optimism, personal intuition, enthusiasm, resilience, compassion, discernment, empathy, persistence, determination, personal balance, kindness, fairness, and so many more. Remember life is 100% what happens to us and 90% how we respond. Our responses to the events, choices, obstacles, and opportunities of our lives originate from our habits.

Choose habits that can lead you where you want to go; choose destiny habits that unlock your unlimited potential; habits that encourage you to spread your wings so that you can SOAR...*s*eek *o*pportunities *a*ctively and *r*ealistically.

Make certain that your habits serve you and that you do not end up serving your habits. Be alert, check your habits and change them when they no longer contribute to the achievement of your dreams. For those habits that impede your progress, check them immediately at the door.

Exercise 2

My Habit Register
Take a closer look at your habits because they
can impact where and how far you can go.

Behavior(s)	Current Habit(s)	Consequences	Steps To Change Habit(s)	Desired Habit	Target Date For Change	Completion Date	Comments

3. Delightfully Disciplined

Sometimes it is so easy to give into our emotions, our fears, our self-doubt. Often, it is so easy to react before thinking; speaking before choosing our words; and acting before considering all the facts. Learning to become more self-disciplined can help you overcome these mental stumbling blocks, and help you develop behaviors that form the basis of lifelong success. Becoming self-disciplined is the art of balancing your emotions with your reasoning.

Simply put, a truly self-disciplined woman considers her feelings and analyzes a situation before taking action. Achieving a happy medium is an important element when deciding the habits, behaviors and choices one wants to embrace. While some might say just use your head, our emotions are powerful and our emotions are a significant driving force that moves us to action. These actions can enable us to transform our dreams into reality, or hinder us without fail. It can sometimes be terribly difficult to control our emotions so learning how to use willpower in those instances will make it possible to make better choices.

Will power and self-discipline are often confused. Willpower is a woman's ability to control her inner unnecessary and sometimes harmful impulses. Willpower is a woman's ability to overcome laziness and procrastination; it is a woman's ability to make a choice, take action and then persevere until she achieves her goal.

Self-discipline is a companion to willpower, and when you find one you tend to find the other. Self-discipline gives a woman the stamina to persist in the face of hardships and challenges; self-discipline helps a woman reject immediate and often fleeting momentary satisfaction for long-term joy.

Self-discipline I am sure is a wonderful thing, the thought of having total control over one's emotions and actions is liberating. Daily, I work to develop more discipline, to consciously consider my choices. I now strive to make my decisions with my eyes wide open, with my spirit fully engaged. I have learned that discipline takes practice, persistence, and a sincere desire to grow. Discipline is learning to master your thoughts and attitudes, understanding who you are, and realizing the things that you do under certain conditions. Strengthening self-discipline is something to work at daily, habit after habit, one action after another, from moment to moment.

Having discipline can aid you when you feel like quitting, when you begin to doubt yourself, when fear is about to paralyze you, when giving up appears to be the only solution. Discipline can give flight to every hope and dream that you possess.

The lack of consistent self-discipline has hindered my progress in so many ways. Although, it has eluded me, I still vigorously pursue it. I still encourage myself to change, and I will become more self-disciplined through sheer determination. Remember self-discipline is a woman's ability to regulate her conduct based upon principle and sound judgment, and not simply by impulse or desire. Strategies to nurture and strengthen your self-discipline include starting with small things, getting your life organized, being aware of and using your time wisely, being punctual, being a woman of your word, doing the most difficult task first, finishing what you start, accepting constructive criticism with a positive attitude, practicing self-denial, and embracing your opportunities to be responsible. Discipline enables a woman to achieve more. In fact, discipline can be an utter delight.

4. Finding Balance

Think of your seven circles of life, think about how you struggle to juggle all of the various aspects of your life, how you work to multi-task each and every day.

Your career is much like a rubber ball. If you drop the career ball, it can generally bounce back. On the other hand, your other circles, family, social, mental, financial, physical and spiritual are more like glass. If you are unsuccessful in your efforts to juggle these dimensions of your life, or perhaps even drop one, things may never be the same.

How many times have you caught yourself saying, "I'd rather be," or "I'd rather do"? Life is too short to shortchange yourself by engaging in work, activities or even relationships that are unfulfilling. Make certain that you have not chosen safe and unsatisfying, instead of seeking challenging and joyful. Make sure that you put as much energy into making a life as you do making a living.

Daily, several friends of mine share that they feel as though something is missing in their lives, something does not feel quite right. I too share their feelings, and I try to put more joy into my life each day. These feelings are typically a symptom of a deeper issue, this unrest points to one's quest and attempt to find life balance.

Remember you have four gifts through which to experience your life: a body, a brain, a heart and a soul. Do some soul searching and find a sense of balance for your life. Reflect daily to make certain that your life represents your values and beliefs, and not someone else's. Find your balance and begin living a soulful, spirit driven life. Nightly, review the activities of your day to determine if you made the best choices among the opportunities that you were presented. By reflecting on your priorities daily, you will learn how to focus your time and energy so that you can meet these priorities, as well as have more time to do all of the things you want to do.

Things to consider as you strive to obtain more balance in today's unbalanced world: remember there is only one of you; identify your priorities; set goals with significant others; treat others the way they want to be treated to minimize stressful interactions; find ways to rejuvenate yourself daily; do not try to be a people pleaser-do what you can-choose to do the things you want to do; schedule and use your time effectively; invest yourself in self-care, other-care and life-care. As you work to achieve more balance in your life, ask yourself the following questions. Which areas of my life are well-balanced? Which areas seem out of balance? What would help bring balance to these areas? Am I willing to make the necessary changes?

5. Stopping Self-Sabotage

Sometimes, I feel like I am getting in my own way. Some days, it seems as though I am my own worse enemy. Have you ever felt that time after time you end up sabotaging yourself? Are you suffering from self-sabotage?

Self-sabotage is the combination of feelings, thoughts and actions that serve as a roadblock to your personal progress and ultimate success. Women who are guilty of self-sabotage always seem to deny themselves pleasure, talk themselves out of taking action because of a fear of failure and an underlying fear of success, and also they undermine their joy and the pursuit of their deepest dreams. Women who sabotage themselves are often attracted to unhealthy relationships, feel that they are unworthy or make dead-end choices because they feel that the possibilities for their lives are limited. Research in this area finds that women with self-defeating behaviors tend to come from homes that were to some extent unloving, inconsistent or unpredictable. Women who score highest on the scale of self-defeating personalities generally perceive their family environments as lacking cohesiveness and being discouraging. While this type of environment can potentially create a great deal of self-doubt, sometimes when a woman chooses to cling to self-sabotage, it is because the events of her past are allowed to dominate her actions of today. What we start with can indeed affect us, that is, until we decide to change it. Check yourself dear sisterfriend, and allow yourself to thrive!!!

Sabotaging Behavior	*Soulful Living Behavior*
• No Purpose or Vision	• Setting and Working Toward Goals
• Lack of Personal Responsibility	• Taking Personal Responsibility
• Negative Attitudes	• Positive Mental Attitudes, Choosing Happiness
• Lack of Awareness	• Taking Initiative to be Informed
• Inability to Communicate Effectively	• Communicating With Others in a Positive Manner
• Inability to Make Choices in Life	• Making Wise Choices About What Goes in Your Mind and Body
• Forming and Maintaining Unhealthy Relationships	• Developing Healthy Relationships with Self and Others

Exercise 3   **Are You Guilty of Self-Sabotage??**

Do you sometimes feel as though you are your own worst enemy? Take the Self-Sabotage Questionnaire and determine if you are sabotaging yourself. Answer every statement with the response that best describes your true behavior. Try to be honest with yourself so that you can begin to identify and change your self-limiting behaviors. Score your responses are follows: Never—0, Rarely—1, Sometimes—2, Often—3, All the Time—4

1. A lot of the people that I spend time with tell me that my ideas are ridiculous.
2. Often, I just want to be someone else, and not myself.
3. I am very afraid to fail at something.
4. I allow my past mistakes and failure to keep me from taking on new tasks or new responsibilities.
5. I find it difficult to accept compliments without minimizing what the person is saying.
6. When I have a challenging project to complete, I expect that I will fail or not be totally successful.
7. I procrastinate a lot and sometimes I miss important deadlines because of this.
8. I tend to be a pessimist; I usually expect that the worse will happen.
9. When I really feel like saying no, I somehow end of saying yes.
10. If I do not do something perfect, then I feel like I have failed completely.
11. As far as I am concerned, I see the glass as being half-empty most of the time.
12. If something goes wrong, I blame others and not myself.
13. I feel like getting even with people who hurt my feelings.
14. When things go wrong, I feel as though it is my responsibility to fix it.
15. I spend more time on other people's problems and not my own.
16. I tend to be my own worse critic.
17. I have difficulty focusing most of the time.
18. When things are going well, I am still uncomfortable and uneasy.
19. It is difficult for me to admit when I have made a mistake.
20. It is hard for me to accept help from others.
21. I feel as though women who go to see therapist are weak.
22. I call myself bad names when I make a mistake or do something wrong.
23. When I have a conflict with someone else, I tend to give in just to keep the peace.
24. I give in to others just to keep the situation from being too stressful.
25. I know that I complain a lot but I cannot seem to stop.

Your Total Score Probably Means: A low score indicates that you tend to undermine yourself very little. A higher score may point to personal behaviors, attitudes and actions that impede your progress.

1-25: Way to Go Girl!!! You tend to self-sabotage yourself very little. You tend to be confident, focused and can handle most challenges that come your way.

26-50: Check Yourself!!!! You are displaying far too many self-sabotaging tendencies.

51-75: Hold Up!!!! You are sabotaging yourself. You are allowing negative self-talk, doubt and fear to hold you back.

76-100: It's Time For Soul Searching!!!! You definitely are a self-saboteur. Analyze your beliefs and determine what habits and attitudes could be holding you back. Work on changing your self-talk and when you find yourself hindering your own progress, stop yourself in your tracks immediately.

6. Developing Diamond Habits

We love to wear them; we love how they shine brilliantly on a cheery, sunny day. Everyone knows that a diamond is a chunk of coal that is transformed into something precious and unique as a result of time and pressure. Everyone knows that diamonds are forever.

Every woman starts out much like that chunk of coal, a simple natural element that has the potential to become an exquisite jewel. You are already a diamond, now you just have to realize the diamond that you are. You might not be sure exactly where you want to be right now, so if that is the case, merely think of yourself as a diamond in the rough, a woman on the verge, a woman on the pathway to, a woman becoming all she can and wants to be.

Develop your diamond habits so that you can weather the passage of time; withstand the pressures of life's good days and bad, still allowing your authentic self to shine through. Remember what you say and what you do is what you get; remember it takes 21 days for a behavior to become a habit. Strengthen the personal habits that make you glitter and reflect the woman that you truly are; use those habits that can take you to the places you want to go. Work to rid yourself of the habits and beliefs that are holding you back, habits that make it difficult for you to achieve your true potential.

Consider integrating these diamond habits into your life:

- ✓ Be clear about what you want
- ✓ Make small changes in your life until they fit comfortably
- ✓ Adjust your attitude as needed every morning before getting out of bed
- ✓ Listen to yourself and monitor your inner voice
- ✓ Pay attention to the tone of your self-talk; quickly plug up your energy leaks (physical spiritual-emotional-mental)
- ✓ Learn to be flexible
- ✓ Be yourself always
- ✓ Use your gifts and talents daily
- ✓ Nurture yourself each day
- ✓ Learn to be grateful for the things you already have
- ✓ Refuse to cling to the past
- ✓ Enjoy your life and embrace your personal journey

- ✓ Life can be humorous so enjoy those moments
- ✓ Live life as though you are on a time clock, you are
- ✓ Create a goal book or a dream book and use it
- ✓ Balance work and play

7. Learn the Lesson

Our life experiences come to teach us, to challenge us, to help us to grow. When we keep failing the same test, keep filling in the blank with the same wrong answer, we have not learned the lesson. In several areas of my life, I have always been challenged, but finally I acknowledged that I was indeed struggling. Those personal declarations have finally empowered me to better embrace change.

If something is not working, change it. If you keep making the same choices when you are faced with the same situations, it's time to look deeper to determine what habits are holding you back. When confronted with challenges or opportunities, analyze all aspects of the situation. Hold fast to the pearls of wisdom that you take from each situation because these life lessons can serve to make you a better woman.

Understand that you will make mistakes sometimes, but not all of the time. Be clear that a mistake is not final until you decide not to correct it. As you work in pursuit of personal success, you will sometimes stumble and fall, mistakes will come. Know that making mistakes is a part of being human. Realize that making mistakes is not an acceptable reason to stop trying. Be mindful that women who achieve will say that their achievements were derived through knowledge gained from their setbacks. Your spirit will be at peace knowing that you sought to accomplish a goal and perhaps encountered mistakes along the way, rather than accepting that you made no attempt to achieve your innermost dreams at all.

Heed your life lessons the first time around, and put this new knowledge into you personal empowerment tool chest. Take this new understanding to heart and use this knowledge to become who you were destined to become. Learn your life lessons and learn them well.

Try this exercise: (1) Write a list of mistakes you've made in your life. (2) From this list, choose one of the mistakes that served as a great teacher for you. Write at least 7 questions that an interested sister friend might want you to answer about this failure. (3) Write an interview with yourself about this mistake, detailing what you learned from this experience. Let your inner spirit ask you the questions that you wrote in Step 2. Allow your inner spirit to ask you the questions that have proven too difficult for you to ask yourself. Take this to heart and begin working to make necessary changes.

Pearls of Wisdom for Soulful Living—Habits

A woman's habits are much like a dandelion. If not nipped at the root in the beginning, they will come back again, again, and again.

A woman who understands her habits has the power to change them.

A woman's habits are generally stronger than reason; knowing this, a woman safeguards her personal space and she chooses her habits carefully

Habits either pave the way, or point out limitations.

Exercise 4   My Belief Tree

Choose four primary roles (wife, mother, daughter, sister, friend, employee, leader, teacher, etc.) that you play in your life and write them in the four boxes in your belief tree. Complete this sentence;" A_____ should" for each of your roles. Write your four answers, your beliefs about each role. Go over each belief and ask yourself the question, "Where did I learn this and why do I still believe it?" Put a star next to the roles and beliefs that are productive and beneficial. Put a check mark besides those roles and beliefs that may be negative habits or self-defeating behaviors that are impacting your life. Decide the steps you will take to change your boulders into diamond habits.

Role 1	Role 2	Role 3	Role 4

Belief 1	Belief 2	Belief 3	Belief 4

Belief 1	Belief 2	Belief 3	Belief 4

Belief 1	Belief 2	Belief 3	Belief 4

Belief 1	Belief 2	Belief 3	Belief 4

Relationships

THE FOURTH KEY TO SOULFUL LIVING

Relationships are an important aspect of a woman's life. Relationships are the interactions we have with others whether on a romantic, friendship, business or blood-related level. Everything that we do involves communicating and relating to others. This can be relationships at work, with family members, with the love of your life, with your children, with your best friend.

In every one of the seven circles of a woman's life, relationships play an important role. While having relationships is key, the quality of these relationships is even more important. Working to develop positive, healthy, mutually supportive relationships is important because the quality of a woman's relationships has a significant impact on other areas of her life.

Far too many women, whether out of a perceived need, fear, self-doubt or other pressures, hold on to relationships that no longer serve any meaningful purpose and actually are more a source of ongoing despair. A woman has got to come to terms with the fact that she must be fully engaged and responsible for the relationships in her life, and she also must have the courage to walk away from relationships that threaten her spirit and her well-being. This walking away should not just be at the drop of a hat because all relationships have their ups and downs. If you do not know it by now, let me share the 411 with you, relationships take work, a lot of it. Walking away should occur when a relationship becomes very painful, when it becomes unpleasantly clear that the other person is not willing to work at improving the quality of the relationship, or when the person does not respect you.

Women tend to play one of four roles in their relationships. These roles are dependent, co-dependent, independent or interdependent. Have you thought about how you function in your relationships? Have you thought about the quality of the relationships in your life and how you can improve them? Are you desperately needy and therefore accept any crumb of attention that others, particularly men throw your way? Do you maintain and pursue relationships whether romantic or friendship wise that you know are negative?

Dependent women feel as though they can accomplish little on their own and that they need other people to do most things for them. Co-dependent women believe that they must first help other people achieve their goals and deal with their issues before taking the time to deal with their own. Independent women feel as though they can achieve everything by themselves just by working hard; they believe that they do not need anyone. Interdependent women feel that they too can achieve their goals through hard work but they also know that they can achieve even more if they give and receive help; these women understand the true power and value of relationships.

How do you function in relationships? Which belief do you hold to be true? Do you have expectations for your relationships? Do you insist that you are treated with respect and dignity in all of your relationships? Do you understand that friendships and romantic relationships should add additional joy to your already satisfying life?

Women who live soulfully realize that relationships are important; they do not enter into new relationships, particularly romantic relationships until they are healed from and have resolved past hurts; women who live soulfully communicate clearly what they want from their relationships, and they also develop healthy relationships with themselves and with others.

Relationships can be a source of immense joy, but the quality of your relationships depends upon what you believe you deserve and the quality of the relationship you have with yourself. Relationship matter, so decide that you will set and maintain standards; be willing to work at creating and maintaining healthy relationships; and you will accept the relationships in your life as they are realizing that you do not control the actions and behaviors of others. Good relationships cannot be developed or carried on the back of one person; good relationships result from the efforts of two people who "try" on a daily basis. Know when to treasure a relationship, and also know when a relationship is not possible.

Key Four Relationships

1. Relationships Do Matter

Relationships are foundations for everything that a woman does in life. A woman's ability to form positive, gratifying, and personally empowering relationships is a critical component of soulful living. Our first exposure to relationships comes in the form of family; then friends, male and female, and eventually significant others. Learning how to interact with others, and being able to develop and maintain healthy relationships is a critical factor for living with serenity.

Sadly, every woman's introduction to relationships is not always pleasant. Sometimes, the people who brought you into the world have their own issues and this makes it difficult for them to serve as role models for healthy relationships. Sometimes, friends do not paint a perfect picture for what constitutes a good friendship either, and too often significant others leave such a trail of misery behind, a woman feels like crawling under a rock for safe cover.

A good start for a woman, regardless of her initial exposure to the world of relationships is to develop a good relationship with herself. It is very difficult to give what you do not have, so having a good relationship with yourself enables a woman to better form healthy relationships with others. This also better equips her to rebound from relationships that prove to be toxic. Having a good relationship with self helps a woman to use her core values to decide upon expectations and boundaries for her relationships with others. Also, when a woman has a good relationship with herself, she has no need to jump into relationships hastily or maintain relationships that are destructive to her spirit.

There are four basic relationships in every woman's life, these are: her relationship with a higher power, whatever your faith; her relationship with self; her relationship with others and her relationship with things. Relationships are either harmonic......that is encouraging, nurturing and productive to the woman's personal growth and happiness; or not harmonic,...that is demeaning, discouraging and disrespectful, ultimately causing the woman a considerable amount of stress, strife and personal power.

Just as you work hard to have positive relationships with yourself and others, make certain that you have a positive viewpoint about materials things. While there is nothing wrong with appreciating nice things or working to acquire them, just remember that things do not validate your self-worth or define you. You are who you are with or without material objects. If by nature you are inconsiderate, you will simply be an inconsiderate person with lot of things. Material things cannot change your character or the content of your heart, only you can.

Seven ways to have powerful relationships with others include:

- ✓ Be Likeable—like yourself and so will other people
- ✓ Remember People's Names—as much as possible, try to remember people's names; people feel special and appreciated when you call them by name
- ✓ Show Others Appreciation—express appreciation for the efforts of others and for their acts of kindness
- ✓ Shower Praise On Others—complement others freely, the more you give, the more you get
- ✓ Listen to What Other People Say and Show Interest—learn to be a good listener; always focus and show genuine interest when having conversations with others
- ✓ Refrain From Criticism—try to be above petty criticism; if you have nothing positive to say, then say nothing
- ✓ Seek Positive Outcomes—always try to end your interactions with others on a positive note

The relationships in a woman's life truly matter, and none of them is more important than the relationship she has with herself. Surround yourself with people who uplift, inspire and cheer you on. If you feel good about your personal relationships, other areas of your life will benefit.

Some soulful living suggestions to enhance the relationships in your life:

- ✓ Make personal relationships a high priority—nurture the ones you have and be open to developing new ones. Life is meant to be shared.
- ✓ Invest time—you devote time to education, work, and the other priorities in your life, also invest in your relationships, this enables your relationships to flourish; spending time in healthy relationships helps to reduce the stress and strains of life
- ✓ Spend time with people you respect and admire—life is too short to hang out with people who bring you down, encourage you to participate in activities you don't approve of, or behave in ways that upset you. Develop relationships with people whom you respect, whose choices you admire, and who inspire you to be all that you can be

- ✓ Work through tensions—unspoken negative feelings can multiply over time; learn to deal with issues in a productive fashion; discuss it, deal with it, move on and let it go
- ✓ Do not tolerate violence—violence is not love; when you tolerate violence out of a belief that it will end, a desire to keep a family together, when your self-esteem is low and you believe that you deserve what you get, or a fear that trying to leave may lead to greater violence, you are only kidding yourself; remember no level of violence is acceptable and be clear in no uncertain terms.... violence is not a form of love
- ✓ Be a good friend—to have a friend be one, be a support system for your friends in good times and bad
- ✓ Take risks and be you—display your true self in all of your relationships
- ✓ If it does not work, learn to cope—everyone experiences strain and breakups in intimate relationships, friendships, and sometimes with family; learn to cope and work to repair the broken relationship as best you can; relationships take work all of the time, everyday

The relationships in a woman's life can be a source of fulfillment or an ongoing source of agony. Choose your relationships carefully, and do not be afraid to fly solo until you find relationships that are right for you.

2. Relationship Readiness

Every woman to ensure that relationships in her life effectively contribute to her well-being must strive to only allow positive relationships into her personal sphere. Women to spare themselves from feelings of hurt, betrayal, disappointment and deceit must learn to take the relationships in their lives more seriously, particularly when it comes to matters of the heart. Romantic relationships, good or bad can impact every aspect of your being. There is nothing like good love, but a woman has got to be willing to find that good love and not just settle for a good time. Good ways to make that happen is for a woman to assess her relationship readiness.

Relationship readiness is being emotionally and spiritually able to form, nurture and maintain friendships, romantic relationships, effective relationships in the workplace, and relationships with family. Relationship readiness means that a woman is not still holding on to hurts and anger from the past. A woman who is relationship ready has healed from childhood pain, failed romantic relationships, disappointing family relationships, and any other relationship experiences that impact her negatively.

Sometimes a woman will enter into a relationship knowing full well that she has not closed the door on her past experiences and by not doing so, she carries a lot of those issues with her into the next relationship. Unfinished business plagues many relationships that on the surface brim with promise. Do not allow loneliness, fear, expectations, peer or family pressure to cause you to involve yourself in a relationship that is counterproductive to your happiness.

Unless you have cleared out the old, it is very difficult to be equipped to handle a new relationship. To be relationship ready, a woman must free herself from the past by allowing herself to naturally grieve. Much like the process of grieving when a loved one passes on, women must allow themselves to grieve the loss of an important relationship. Allow yourself to move from feelings of shock, denial, anger, depression, understanding and finally acceptance. Once you allow yourself the time to bring closure to an ended relationship, you are better able to heal and love again.

Before beginning a new romantic relationship, make certain that you are ready. Make it a point to work on strengthening all of the relationships in your life daily. Be courageous and journey through you past relationships; identify what went wrong and what went right; reconcile the past and let it go. By doing so, you will free yourself to fully love others right now, in the present.

Assess your readiness before beginning yet another relationship that becomes posed to fail under the weight of excess emotional baggage. Relationship readiness is your personal ticket to relationship fulfillment, so make sure you are ready before getting on board.

Exercise 1

A Woman's Soulful Living Relationship Readiness Quiz

Answer these questions with a True or False response and find out if you are ready for a committed relationship.

1. I feel strong in my identity as a single person and already have a tremendously fulfilling life.
2. A committed relationship would be a wonderful addition to my life but is not something I must have to feel complete as a woman.
3. My finances and legal matters are in order.
4. My relationships with my parents, ex-partners, children, siblings and extended family are functional and will not interfere with me having the life and relationship that I want.
5. I am in a stable place in my life, and I do not anticipate making any major life changes right now.
6. I am available for a committed relationship, and I have no unfinished relationship business that would interfere with developing and maintaining a committed relationship.
7. I am emotionally and psychologically ready for a partnership.
8. I feel as though I am self-aware and I work on an ongoing basis to deal with any personal issues that might impact my ability to maintain an intimate partnership.
9. My work life and my work schedule would not be an obstacle to a relationship.
10. I have no physical health issues that would make starting a new relationship a challenge.

Relationship Quiz Scoring

10 TRUE answers: You probably have already attracted a partner or are not interested in a relationship right now
9 TRUE answers: You are definitely ready for a relationship
8 TRUE answers: You are probably ready, so open up your heart
7 TRUE answers: You are ready to love again
6 TRUE answers: You may want to work on the areas that need attention before beginning a new relationship
5 TRUE answers: You might need to do some self-development work before getting into another relationship

4   TRUE answers: You definitely need to pursue some self-development work before jumping into another relationship
3   TRUE answers: You are not ready and need to do some personal reflection
2   TRUE answers: Seek some help and allow yourself to heal before starting another relationship
1   TRUE answers: Learn to love yourself before trying to love someone else
0   TRUE answers: A relationship is the last thing you should be thinking about

3. Accepting People As They Are

One of the most difficult things for people to do, particularly women is to accept people as they are. Take a moment and think about the relationships you have at work, with family and friends, with the love of your life, and then ask yourself the question, do I accept these people as they are?

People that we have relationships with tell us and show us who they are in various ways, but we as women often walk around with the notion that somehow the behaviors of others are because of us. Sometimes we feel as though if we look or act differently, talk differently or change something about ourselves, the person that we have the relationship with will somehow magically change.

The reality of this matter is that from the moment we meet a person, they provide us with snapshots of the person that they are, and even when we see who they are, we often refuse to believe. When people demonstrate to us who they are we are faced with two choices, one is to accept that person with all of their strengths and imperfections and be prepared to deal with any consequences that may result from their actions and behaviors; or simply run not walk away if we know that we simply do not want to deal with the difficulties a relationship with this person might bring. This is why it is so critical for a woman to define her expectations and value systems when it comes to relationships because people will treat us as we allow.

Learning to accept people as they are is extremely important when it comes to matters of the heart. If you think that your love can somehow change an emotionally distant man, if you think that your love can make a womanizer stop playing with women's emotions, if you think that your love can stop the pain dished out by a violent man, if you think that your love can cure your loved one's drug addiction, then you are sadly mistaken. While your love can make someone want to change and certainly may serve as a catalyst leading to a change in behavior, you must clearly understand that people do not change who they are until they decide that they want to become someone different. It is a powerful testament to their love for you if the person realizes that they need to change to remain in your life, but for the change to be long lasting it is best when that person initiates the change.

As I was about to get married the first time, I clearly remember when it was time for me to say "I Do" I hesitated as I heard a voice clearly say do not do this.

In retrospect I believe that it was my inner spirit trying to protect me from myself. Still, I pressed on. I pressed on believing that our love, my love could combat, could change what my soul already knew. There had been signs all along the way that the person I was about to start sharing my life with was not the man for me. Sensing that something was not right, I refused to relent and on a sunny Valentine's Day morn in the Caribbean, I jumped the broom. Perhaps at the time I felt an overwhelming need to be married, maybe I felt that time was running out, maybe it was just reckless behavior. Even though deep within I knew who and what this man was, I shook off all of my doubt, smiled warmly and uttered the works "I Do." During our brief marriage my initial suspicions proved to be true, and after two years of pain, stress, embarrassment and little joy I left.

As I reflect back on other relationships, I now see that each time the person told me who they were and even with that knowledge I refused to see and accept that fact until pain enveloped me. Was I suffering from low self-esteem, hunger for a relationship? Was I ready for a relationship? Did I even know what I wanted and needed in a relationship? These are the questions that you must ask yourself before playing relationship roulette.

I now know that because I would not learn the lesson, this sad song kept replaying until I acknowledged that as powerful as I may feel in other areas of my life, I do not have the power to change people. This scenario kept repeating until I grew to understand that I must accept people for whom they are and then consciously decide if I want to allow that person into my personal space, into this treasure chest I call my life.

Be clear about your relationships. Be certain that you are not confusing the person's actual behaviors, attitudes and values with the ideal that you have created in your mind and your heart.

Relationships are at the very core of everything a woman does in all seven circles of her life, so make certain that you are not sleeping with the enemy, sharing meals with someone out to sabotage you, or loving someone who does not understand the meaning of the word. Pay attention to what people do, not what they say.

Assess your relationships.

My Relationship Assessment

Person You Have the Relationship With	Relationship Strengths	Areas of the Relationship That Need Work	Strategies You Will Take to Improve The Relationship	Can You This Relationship Be Saved?

4. Feeling Your Heart

Most of the best things in life can not been seen with the naked eye, or experienced through the power of touch. To truly experience the wonder of some things, they must be felt with the heart.

A lot of times, there is a mismatch between the understandings that emanate from our mind and our heart. Sometimes even though we see something happening, we still do not believe what is going on at the time. Much like when a storm brews in the sky and the beauty of the sky becomes hidden from our sight; at the time we only see the storm. But once the storm has subsided, the beautiful sky returns for us to enjoy. This is much like the mind and heart game we play daily. We see harsh realities with our mind and pleasing blue skies with our heart. Consider how a newborn baby feels safe when his or her mother is nearby. This is because the baby is experiencing that moment through the heart not the mind. The newborn is not concerned about safety because the heart is calm simply by feeling the mother's presence.

We are free when our hearts are unbounded, so learning to have heartfelt experiences and developing heartfelt relationships is important for creating this kind of inner peace and joy. Our understanding comes from our hearts and not from our minds. When we allow our minds to make us selfish, our hearts will work to make us generous. While our mind can help us to make decisions, our heart allows us to touch and feel other hearts and in the end make a more complete decision.

Try to always think from your heart before making any decision, for your mind is part of the human body, but your heart is part of, at the core of your divine soul. Sometimes it is very difficult to articulate what your heart truly feels because your mind attempts to keep this emotional side of our being in check. When we are sad and we shed tears of agony, although the tears fall from our eyes, we are really crying in our hearts, crying from the depths of our souls.

Roberta Sage Hamilton, a writer says, "In our deepest moments of struggle, frustration, fear, and confusion, we are being called upon to reach in and touch our hearts. Then, we will know what to do, what to say, how to be. What is right is always in our deepest heart of hearts. It is from the deepest part of our hearts that we are capable of reaching out and touching another human being. It is, after all, one heart touching another heart."

To enjoy a heartfelt life you must be clear about it contents. Know what you desire, and seek it. Feeling your heart enables you to stay in tune with your interests, your creativity, and your motivation.

In your relationships, as well as in all seven circles of your life, reflect often as follows:

1. **I know what I want:** I have a clear vision for my life and my relationships. I can envision my perfect life in rich detail and this makes me feel strong and keeps me motivated.
2. **I know my values and requirements:** I have a written list of at least seven non-negotiable requirements that I use for screening potential partners. I am clear that if any are missing, a relationship will not work for me. I have written requirements or goals for all seven circles of my life.
3. **I am happy with me:** I enjoy my life, my work, my family, my friends, and my own company. I am living the life that I want and my relationships only serve to enhance my life. If single, I will not seek a relationship out of desperation and need.
4. **I am satisfied with my work/career:** My work is fulfilling, and supports my lifestyle.
5. **I am healthy mind, body, and spirit:** My physical, mental, or emotional health does not interfere with my ability to enjoy life.
6. **I have established my financial and success goals:** I am working to achieve the financial goals that I have set for myself, and I have a healthy attitude about success and material things.
7. **I have effective relationship skills:** I understand relationships, can maintain closeness and intimacy, communicate authentically and assertively, negotiate differences positively, allow myself to trust and be vulnerable, and can give and receive love without emotional barriers.

Remember a change of heart can change almost anything!!!

5. Saying I Do To Your Soul

Finding the courage to embrace your true personality, your dreams, and the life that you want to lead at times may seem overwhelming. For most women, work, the demands of family, day-to-day living, perhaps children or other responsibilities make the thought of having your ideal life seem virtually impossible. I challenge you to think about your life in another fashion. By working to create the life that your soul beckons you to lead, a woman can derive spill over benefits in other areas of her life. I dare say that the more a woman is able to focus and pursue her passions, the more goodness she is able to give to her family, her friends, her children, to herself.

Far too many women go through life with feelings of dread, little joy and an underlying sadness. Much of this can be attributed to never getting in touch with their very essence, their soul. Finding work that you enjoy, sharing your life with people that bring positive energy into your life, and immersing yourself in the mesmerizing wonder of each day can bring so much added stimulation to your life and your spirit.

Saying I do to your soul is finding your true calling and doing it. Saying I do to your soul is being grateful for all that you already have and opening yourself up to receive additional blessings. Saying I do to your soul is learning to trust your dreams and being willing to pursue them. Saying I do to your soul is learning to pamper yourself and not feeling guilty about taking time for you.

Saying I do to your soul is loving all of your "self" while working to improve the things you want to change. Saying I do to your soul is refusing to settle, refusing to give up, and refusing to dishonor the uniqueness of you.

6. The Power of Forgiveness

Imagine walking through life with a hundred pound bag of mangoes on your back. Wonder if you had to sleep with this burden, bathe with it; sit down at the table for a snack with it attached securely to your back. Sooner than later, most of us would find a way to rid ourselves of such a limiting burden. Although some of us may not realize it, but that is exactly how we are living our lives daily, weighed down by baggage that we simply refuse to discard. Far too many of us are journeying through life carrying the emotional and psychological anguish, strain, stress and strife from numerous past hurts.

Whether it is anger, resentment or bitterness against a parent, relative, mate or friend that has wronged us in the past, the past is long gone and the only thing it can do for you now is teach you how to live better in the present, and "mo better" in the future. Holding on to negative attitudes, feelings and experiences have a direct affect on our health, well-being and ability to personally flourish. Learning to forgive both others and ourselves is one of the most powerful personal traits a person can possess. The power to forgive gives way to personal resiliency, and this characteristic enables us to move forward even in the face of life's inevitable challenges.

Granted, we are all products of our life experiences and our personal histories. Further, we can easily allow these past events to impact our current thoughts and feelings in either a positive or negative manner. If we allow it to fester, unpleasant, unfair and unkind actions by others can remain in our minds and spirits for a lifetime. People, even those who say they love and care for you, can sometimes be cruel, and this treatment may in fact dictate anger on your part. The trick is to communicate your anger in a healthy manner, find some way in your heart to forgive the person and then move on. Being upset is not the problem; the problem lies in never letting the issue go, choosing to relive the event over and over.

Each of us has a choice to make, do I stay "stuck in the mud," or do I choose to move on and "enjoy the gift of life and the beauty of the sunshine each day."

The power of forgiveness sets our minds, souls and spirits free. Whether we realize it or not, it takes more energy to maintain the anger than it does to resolve the matter. We must learn to rid ourselves of the negative and unproductive feelings that hold us back from the blessings that seek to come our way.

Bitterness is a dangerous destructive force that can eat away at your very spiritual core. Don't stifle your life or block your blessings because you refuse to forgive others. The inability to forgive destroys people and relationships, and it can make us prisoners of our hurts and hatred.

Decide today to wipe the slate clean, even if it means that you take the first step. Let all of that old bitterness go, and unleash the undeniable power of forgiveness into your life.

7. Do You Hear What I Am Saying

A critical aspect of relationships and life in general is the ability to communicate what you are feeling and what you want. Some times we as women act as though people can read our minds or already know our needs. Unfortunately, this is not the case. It may be a litter scary to step out on a limb, open up and tell people what you are feeling, but if you do not, how will they know. How can you expect someone to hear what you are saying if you do not utter a word?

Communicating your needs and wants help to clear the air and minimizes confusion. Think about it for a moment, do you feel as though you truly understand what your significant other wants from you? How about your boss or your employees? Can you clearly articulate what you want from them?

Good communication is at the heart of good relationships and good relationships are the basis for soulful living. Learn how to express your innermost thoughts without fear or hesitation; learn to be a good listener so that your communication with others can improve. Get in the habit of articulating your feelings in a productive, non-critical fashion. Even so, also learn to express your anger and disappointment but do not allow it to fester in your spirit and do not harbor it in your heart.

If communicating your feelings is a little difficult, work to master these seven steps so that your ability to communicate with others will improve. (1) prepare—think about the points you want to make, prepare notes if necessary; (2) listen—listen intently to what the other person is saying and accept their point of view even if you do not agree, after all everyone has an opinion; (3) read—analyze the situation and determine how best to proceed; (4) gain attention—reiterate the points that you want to make; (5) declare—be specific about what you want or need; (6) interpret—determine if the person clearly understands your point of view; (7) ask for action—urge the person to make changes that will improve the situation for both of you. Mastering these seven steps can help you improve your communication with others.

Try this exercise with your husband, your boyfriend, a family member, your child, even your best friend.

List your answers to these two simple questions and then discuss your responses in a quiet, soothing setting. You might be surprised by the other person's responses, but these responses I am certain will go a long way to improving your relationship.

1. What do I want, or want more of, from_____?
2. What I don't want, or want less of from_____?

Pearls of Wisdom for Soulful Living—Relationships

Find peace within yourself and then you can share it with others.

The quality of your relationships is intricately tied to your expectations.

Our relationships teach us who we are, what we need and how to love.

Relationships are meant to expand our world not define it.

A relationship cannot make you feel whole, if inside you feel shattered to pieces.

If you cannot bear to be along, you are not ready to seek a relationship. Loneliness is a state of mind that can be present whether in a relationship or if you are flying solo.

Faith

THE FIFTH KEY TO SOULFUL LIVING

Considering the troubled times in which we currently live, without some kind of solid spiritual foundation to cling to, navigating life and its challenges from day to day will prove extremely difficult.

Each woman will travel her own unique journey to faith, but trust me; sooner or later you will get there. Whether it is a result of a heartbreaking relationship, a sick loved one, problems at the job, a child that will not listen, health problems of your own, abuse by a family member or a mate, unrealized dreams, or countless disappointments, one day your spirit will cry out for it, one day you will have a test of faith and you will search for it.

Daily miracles abound all around us, and these are the work of the Creator. Daily, circumstances and situations help women around the globe find their faith. Daily, women develop a deeper understanding of the power and wonder of faith as the yearnings of their heart come to fruition. Sometimes a woman does not even know how or why. Daily, in those quiet moments when a woman ponders her deepest thoughts, she cries out for comfort, for the strength to go on.

To accomplish your dreams, to believe that these dreams are even possible, a woman must have faith. To find joy in living during both good and bad times, a woman must have faith. To achieve inner peace and learn how to maintain serenity and calmness when the seas of life get rough, a woman must have faith. To overcome doubt, fear and personal pain, a woman must have faith.

My journey to faith has been painful, but this journey has made me a stronger woman. This journey has helped me to become more self-aware. My discovery of the power of faith has come through tumultuous friendships, painful romantic relationships, dealing with the diagnosis of my mother's cancer, watching my father struggle with the effects of diabetes, seeing my sister battle with her personal demons, watching my husband work to get in touch with himself while trying to forgive himself for past mistakes, and my own efforts to deal with the consequences of my many choices, far too many of which were poor choices to say the least.

What I now know is that if a woman is not spiritually grounded, she will flounder. What I now know is that if a woman does not have faith, she will spend her entire life unfulfilled and discontented. What I now know is that without enduring faith, a woman will accomplish little and her spirit will suffer very much. There will come a moment in time when you will need unwavering faith to pull you through. This moment may come in the form of a big dream that requires all the faith you can muster to achieve it; this moment may come in the way of a personal challenge, a family crisis, or a life dilemma.

Do not confuse the question of religion, with matters of faith. Do not confuse your need to develop a relationship with the Creator with the chaos at the local church. Faith is knowing that the Creator intended for you to have the things in your heart, and once you believe these things possible, they will be. You cannot travel the life path without a fountain of faith, and the sooner you realize this, the more joyful your life travels will be. When doubt tries to overtake you, have faith, for through your faith, all things are possible. Allow your faith to grow…

Key Five Faith

1. Following An Invisible Trail Home

Planted inside of every woman is a fountain of potential, numerous possibilities. Through faith, a woman is able to tap into that watershed of opportunities, which are presented to her. By planting her seeds and working hard, a woman can manifest this potential to create the outcomes that she desires.

What is faith? Faith is respecting the Creator's ability. Faith is your conviction. Faith is having assurances that what you desire will occur. Faith is the certainty that what you hope for you believe that it will be. Faith is a source of strength for when the going gets rough. Faith is taking the only one step that a woman can take and that is the one in front of her.

A lot of women do not understand faith and really do not truly see its purpose. Faith is the cornerstone of a strong belief system, a sense that no matter how bad things may seem or how dark the cloud might appear, in the end everything will be all right. Faith is a belief that can help you combat feelings of doubt and fear; it can help you overcome feelings that you have no control over the situations that comprise your life.

Our lives become stressful when we feel as though we do not know what to do. These feelings, particularly without a sense of faith, make us lose confidence in our abilities to move forward. This lack of faith makes us feel helpless, make us feel like crying out for help.

Few of us probably have much confidence in believing things that we cannot see. Few of us would probably put much stock in following an invisible trail anywhere. But a woman must somehow get beyond the limitations of her mind and realize that there is an extraordinary invisible trail at her disposal courtesy of the Creator. Faith is available to support a woman in everything that she attempts to do, that is, if a woman chooses to call upon faith to accompany her.

Faith trails exist to help us cross through and cross over to the land of possibilities. Faith trails exist as support systems to help us "keep on keeping on" when our minds and spirits tell us to give up. Faith trails are there to encourage us to get up when we fall, to keep growing when we are challenged, and to become stronger mind, body and spirit knowing that the Creator is always there for us.

What is faith? Faith is through it all following an invisible trail home, and home is where your divine spirit seeks to take you. Faith is believing even before you are able to see IT, touch IT, be IT, whatever your IT may be.

2. Hold On…It's Coming

Your job is unsatisfying because your dream is to own a business. You seem to be unlucky in love because your latest relationship has turned into a dead end, another heartbreak. You have a burning desire to do something different with your life but you are torn between sticking with what you know and pursuing what you really want.

Sowing seeds for your dreams is something that you owe to yourself. Even when it might appear that you cannot possibly achieve your goal, you have to hold on, because if your faith is in check, you know that it is just a matter of time before success is yours. You have to hold on because it's coming. You have to look past the challenges of the moment onward to the day you savor the sweet taste of success. You have to hold on because through your persistence what you want is on the way.

It is so easy to allow yourself to get caught up in the melee of the moment. It is so easy to lose sight of things that we really want, and to give up on our dreams before we even attempt to pursue them. Unless a woman actively seeks to answer the callings of her spirit, she will feel a restlessness; a thirst that she cannot quench. Choosing to live a life dominated by "settling" will only make a woman discouraged and overtime make her spiritually bankrupt.

Ask yourself daily, what kind of seeds am I sowing? What am I seriously doing to pursue my dreams and improve the quality of my life? What am I doing about my seven circles of life goals and objectives?

Through my own struggles and search for more joy in my life, I have gained a keen understanding of the harvest principle. The harvest principle is based upon four basic laws:

Law Number One—You Reap Only If You Sow

In this life, you do not get something for nothing; you must put out some effort to achieve your dreams. You have to try one step at a time, day by day. If you do very little, very little will come your way. In this life, we indeed reap what we sow.

Law Number Two—You Will Reap What You Sow

In this life, you get what you give. If you sow seeds of pessimism, negativity and ill will that is what you will receive in return. The words that we speak and the actions that we take return to us in the same fashion. So sow well and walk good. Your life depends upon it.

Law Number Three—You Will Always Reap More Than You Sow

In this life, the effort that we make, the steps that we take are multiplied by the Creator. We always get back much more than what we begin with. Fill yourself with optimism daily as you pursue your life goals and your calling. For this, your personal rewards will be great, and your talents will multiply.

Law Number Four—You Always Reap After You Sow

In this life, all of the benefits, joy and success that you seek will come after you have taken the time and demonstrated to the Creator that what you speak is genuinely what you aspire to achieve. Just as the harvest comes after the seeds are sown, and joy cometh after the storm, once you plant your dream seeds in fertile ground, your abundance will come.

I have found that to manifest the goodness of the harvest principle in your life one must obey these four laws. Also, understand that with sincere faith and persistence, the harvest principle will manifest itself through a series of stages.

The first is the believing season; this is when a woman grows to know herself and becomes in tune with her calling and her spirit. Next, comes the vision season. This is when a woman creates a vision for her life reflecting her personal calling, her values, her gifts and talents.

The preparatory season is a time for a woman to plan, make contacts, network, form a support system and identify the actions that it will take to achieve her vision. Now, she is ready for the sowing season. This is a time to begin putting her plans into action; a time to begin the process of making her heart's desire a reality. During the nurturing season, a woman must work hard to achieve her goals. Perseverance, patience, and prayer will see a woman through the nurturing season. Through her faith, a woman will soon reach the harvest season; and this is the time for a woman to rejoice because she has finally achieved her dream. The thanksgiving season is the last stage of the harvest principle. The thanksgiving season is a glorious time for this is when a woman celebrates all of the blessings that she has received; this is a time for her to share her blessings with others; a time to show her gratitude for all the good seeds that have converged and sprouted to bring her success.

Always stay focused on your dreams and not the temporary challenges that come your way. Why? Because all you have to do is to persist, for what you seek is waiting for your arrival.

3. And This Too Shall Pass

Deep down you may feel hurt, disappointed and dismayed. You feel as though you cannot cry. There is so much pain, yet there are no tears. No tears to wet your eyes, just the pain, more and more of it. You feel as though the agony of the obstacles that you face will never end. Bouts of pain become all that you know.

Pain is the wound that the soul carries on the inside. The extent of the damage cannot be seen, but it is there. In the absence of soul searching and faith, the wound may never heal. This torment can become a part of your soul, a part of your very being if you allow that to happen. The torment lingers as a woman grows from a baby, to a child, a teenager, and finally an adult. If she is not careful, a woman can spend a lifetime haunted by poor choices, bad decisions, missed opportunities, unhealthy relationships; words spoken in anger.

It seems as though memories, reflections, hindsight, revelations, and spiritual awakenings can lead to greater understanding and deeper capacities for perseverance. This spiritual awakening is not possible until a woman realizes that although the storms of life will come, joy always cometh in the morning.

A lasting spiritual awakening will not come until a woman achieves a personal balance that includes the knowledge that no matter what trouble comes her way, storms only lasts for a time. Come what may; always remember that whatever the difficulties you face they too will pass. As are the seasons of nature, and just as night gives way to day, things change, and nothing stays the same forever.

Mental and spiritual freedom will come if you endure. Endurance brings eventual personal jubilation. A spiritual dance of joy, peace, letting it all go occurs and the inner child that resides within you is finally calmed. The pain and wounds are healed. With this blossoming comes a higher level of faith, and now you are free to become, to do what your heart desires.

You cannot allow the storms of life to cause you to stray away from your intended divine destination. Recognize that indeed everything that you need to achieve your personal vision is already inside of you and is merely waiting to be acknowledged by you. Know that possibilities unrecognized by you are not celebrated. Understand that talents unused too often become talents lost. Your personal resolve must be stronger than perceived stumbling blocks. If not, you will be more prone to allow setbacks to stifle your efforts or make you quit.

While you may experience a few bumps along the way, remember, "trouble don't last always", and when it does come, it will pass leaving a stronger woman behind.

Exercise 1   A Test of Faith

Think about events that have occurred in your life. Consider how you responded and how you could have responded to the situation. List ways that you demonstrated your faith in that situation. Also, list actions that you can take in the future to strengthen your personal faith when faced with the same or similar challenges again.

The Event	How I Responded	Did I Demonstrate Faith	Ways I Can Improve My Faith

Exercise 2   The Harvest Principle

Put the Harvest Principle to work in your life. Using one of your goals or dreams, define what each season means to you and think about the actions that you must take to achieve your goal. Think about what success during each season means to you. This exercise will help you to remember that everything you want to achieve is a process, and if you persist you will ultimately prevail.

My Personal Goal/My Personal Dream

The Season	What This Season Means To Me	The Actions I Need To Take	How I Will Measure My Success
Believing Season			
Vision Season			
Preparatory Season			
Sowing Season			
Nurturing Season			
Harvest Season			
Thanksgiving Season			

4. Go On

A very ill mother suffering from cancer and it pains me to watch her as I wish that I could make things better; a father battling the debilitating effects of diabetes and I see a sadness in his eyes as he is no longer able to be the active person that he always was before this; a sister who is struggling desperately to find herself and reclaim her spirit; a job that pays some of the bills but does not allow me to pursue my passion; more bills than money every month; no strong personal support system but lots of calls from family and friends seeking support; a marriage burdened down with emotional and personal baggage from days gone by; health issues of my own that do not get their proper attention because I put myself last; failing to take the time to care for me; longing to return to live in a place that I love, a place that I left after loosing everything that I owned twice because of deadly hurricanes; living a life that is not the life of my dreams but a life that is mine nonetheless because of my choices; far too many unfulfilled dreams; and a brooding deep sadness that is hidden fairly well from the people I meet.

Day by day, this is how I begin my day, overwhelmed by the sickness, sadness and disappointment that surround me. Some days just finding a quiet corner and weeping feels far more appropriate that starting the day. Some days, it is hard to focus, to concentrate on much of anything because my thoughts of the struggles that loved ones and friends face overtakes me. Yet, in the face of it all, I put one foot in front of the other and I go on each and every day.

At first, I approached pressing on half-heartedly. I did not have the luxury of stopping and although I continued to move through my day, neither my head nor my heart was in it. On day, while watching the sunset, as a orange-red globe of light slithered into the sea, I shed a tear. On the back of a refreshing tropical breeze I heard a voice clearly say, "Hold on to your faith, do not give up, I will always be with you." I looked around because I thought that perhaps it was my husband speaking to me, but it was not him; he was still jogging down the beach.

The voice spoke in a calming tone and in a matter of seconds, the emotional load that I had been feeling disappeared. In that moment, I realize that the Creator had spoken to me in my time of despair. From that day, even though few things have changed in my life, my ability to handle it and have faith that everything will be all right has improved. My attitude has shifted back to one of hope and optimism, a viewpoint that I had lost. I have decided to choose happiness and to relish each day and continue to go on. I have traded in doubt and anxiety for trust and belief, fear and worry for courage and acceptance, disappointment and sadness for anticipation and joy.

No matter what you are facing, no matter what you are going through, our life experiences come to teach us, they come to prepare us for our next exciting opportunity. When your life storms come, remain prayerful and stay focused on your goals. No matter what, no matter, never loose sight of the fact that you must go on and you can.

Exercise 3

What Is Life Trying To Teach Me???

Think about events that have occurred in your life. Think about how these temporary setbacks and challenges have taught you some valuable lessons that have made you a stronger and a better person.

Event	What I Learned	How I Used That Lesson To Grow Stronger

5. You Can Make It Happen If You Only Believe

Quitting is the only way that you will fail. There, its been said, and now you are free to press on. If only it was that easy. Well it can be if only you believe. That is, a deep inner belief that what you want to accomplish can and will be done.

Our words are powerful. Whether spoken aloud or in the mental discussions that a woman has with herself all day long, a woman's words can either reinforce her faith, bolster her belief, or tear it all to shreds.

A woman's belief system is indeed the cornerstone of her faith, and contrary to what some people think, no woman is faithless. Be clear that the question is not whether we possess faith. The real question is where a woman places that faith. A woman's thoughts serve as a good barometer of the object of her faith. These thoughts, a woman's beliefs color her view of the world, as well as reflect her attitude about her chances to be victorious in her endeavors.

Our faith is a process that helps us release life-changing power in either a positive or negative direction. For instance, think how much more depressed you feel after verbally expressing that thought. Think about how your feelings of tiredness increase after saying how tired you feel after a brief yawn. In the book of Proverbs, it is written "Death and life are in the power of the tongue." This tells us that our true beliefs are spoken from our lips, and these words impact our beliefs down to the core. These words tell us that we can speak life or despair into our lives.

There is a growing acceptance that 75 to 90 percent of all illnesses result from the body's response to stress. Stress comes from our thoughts, our beliefs, and an absence of faith. When a woman allows life-draining emotions like anger, anxiety, guilt, fear and sadness to become the dominant forces controlling her emotions, she is inviting death and disease into her life, she is systematically crushing her dreams. She is creating her own dis–ease.

Too often a woman will express a belief that she can achieve her goals. In another second, she is speaking words of doubt. A woman has to develop an everlasting belief and faith in herself. Her intention to accomplish a goal must be strong. A woman must be able to hold fast to her dreams in the face of difficulties, and believe that she has vast opportunities and a genuine ability to be successful.

Sincere belief is the primary ingredient for creating genuine faith. If you do not totally believe that you can achieve your aim, how can you solicit the support of others? How will you be able to motivate yourself to press on regardless if you are filled with so much uncertainty?

You have been given the power to accomplish your goals and to live a soul-filled life; that power starts with the extent of your belief. Your personal power is in your mind, in your thoughts. To achieve what you want, you have to believe.

6. Digging Deeper

Are you living a superficial life? Are you perpetrating a fraud by not revealing the real you? Do you give others the impression that you are immensely happy and that you are thoroughly enjoying your life? Do you think about your life-long dreams from time to time, but put little effort into pursuing them because you simply have too many responsibilities to take a chance on your dreams? Do you do things that you do not want to do or say yes to people and commitments that you are not interested in because you do not want to make waves?

I have lived such a life for far too long. I have silently suffered while my spirit has cried out to be heard.

My quest to dig deeper started on September 15, 1995. I sat curled up in a closet as a hurricane ravished the island on which I lived. I could hear the wind howling, debris crashing against the house, and the thrashing of palm and mango trees breaking into pieces. There was no electricity or telephone service because the storm had knocked out the lines.

While my husband slept, I listened to water flow into the house. After all, one portion of the house had been neatly stripped away and was no longer able to contain the water. We were forced to take refuge in the closet. I wondered if we were going to survive. We did. That brush with death, the first of two others, has made me develop a deeper appreciation for life and an urgent need to live my calling.

My attempts to live a more authentic life have forced me to go places that I would much rather not go. My digging deeper has forced me to take a close look at myself and come to grips with all of my strengths, but particularly my weaknesses. I have had to deal with the unresolved concerns of my inner child; I have had to bring closure to issues still remaining from negative relationships and friendship that have long ended. I have finally forgiven myself for poor choices and wasted opportunities. It can be painful to take a honest look at yourself, but in the end you will be able to work through it and you will be glad that you went through such a tumultuous process. Digging deeper is the only way that a woman can rid herself of the mental, spiritual and psychological burdens that are holding her back. This is the only way that a woman can stop making excuses and start taking proactive actions necessary to make desired life changes.

Travel to your inner spaces, dust out those tight emotional corners, and sweep your spirit clean of energy blockers you find there. Try this exercise and begin to dig deeper. Dig deeper to find greater personal awareness, increased faith and new beginnings; dig deeper so that you can discover the real you.

Exercise 4

Things I hate to admit about myself	Why I hate to admit this	What belief do I hold that contributes to this	What does this say about my faith	How can I stop this and start living in a more positive manner

7. Inner Trust

A woman gets what she expects, and her expectations are so tied to her vision, beliefs, values, attitude, actions, faith, and persistence.

Learning to trust your spirit is a different process for every woman. The more spiritually aware a woman becomes, the more she will be able to hear her inner guide. We get what we expect out of life. So, a woman must work to keep her expectations high and her faith strong. A woman must expect to find what she is looking for, expect to achieve what she is aiming for, and expect to enjoy what she receives.

The ideas that form your divine dreams are planted in your heart by the Creator. Ideas are given to us to solve a problem, and to serve as a blessing to others. Good ideas are generally very interesting ideas, but divine ideas are those ideas that wake you in the middle of the night. Divine ideas are those ideas that turn into a personal obsession. Recognizing and developing inner trust helps a woman to take these ideas and grow them into powerful vessels of change.

There are seven facts about ideas that a woman must always remember. Understanding these facts enables a woman to better hear and trust the ideas that come from her spirit.

- **Divine ideas come from the observations that you make regarding the things around you**
- **Divine ideas are concepts and things to help other people**
- **Divine ideas help someone solve a problem**
- **Divine ideas serve to reduce stress while increasing joy and inner peace**
- **Divine ideas may not always be respected and appreciated by people around you so this is why personal belief and faith are so important; the world would have lost the benefit of numerous advances if the person with the idea had given up because of another person's doubt**
- **Divine ideas can create divine wealth and can provide a lifetime of personal satisfaction for you**
- **Divine ideas demand unique and sustained attention in order to fully achieve them**

No matter how things may appear, no matter the threat of a possible failure, even multiple failures. Remember, you are always only one idea away from achieving your ultimate goal, but first you must learn how to trust your ideas and your ability. Inner trust can guide and direct you, but first you must learn the art of listening and the practice of faith.

Pearls of Wisdom for Soulful Living—Faith

> A woman must learn to believe some things before she actually sees them.
>
> Faith is listening to your spirit, heeding the call of your soul, and understanding that goodness is yours for the mere asking.
>
> Through faith, a woman learns that although storms may come, she will weather them, and she will prevail.
>
> The invisible becomes the possible; the possible becomes the incredible through a woman's deep and abiding faith.
>
> A woman's faith is not what she knows but what she chooses to believe.
>
> A woman is a reflection of her faith, for a woman cannot exceed and become more than her capacity to believe.
>
> The tests of life will come, but faith will help you pass every test that comes your way.
>
> If you are going to make it happen, first you must believe.
>
> If failure was not even a possibility, the thing that you would do without hesitation is a faith trail trying to lead you to your destiny.

Courage

THE SIXTH KEY TO SOULFUL LIVING

Sooner or later, a woman will ask herself the questions, "What does it take, just what does it take?" Does it take raw intelligence, education at the best schools, truck loads of money, extraordinary talent, knowing all the right doors to open, or maybe all the right questions to ask? How can I go on when I feel humiliated, like a failure, disappointed in myself? How can I press on when I am afraid? As she ponders these questions, it will become clear that what a woman needs is courage: tenacity, mettle, fortitude, bravery, resolve and boldness.

Poet Maya Angelou writes, "Courage is the most important of all virtues, because without it we can't practice any other virtue with consistency."

Without courage, it is difficult for a woman to move forward in her life with any definiteness of purpose. Talent and ability will not be enough if a woman does not have courage to act upon them. Nothing will be enough without the courage to take that first step, because taking that first step can give a woman the courage to take another step. This show of courage leads to greater faith. Without question, the choice to live life on your own terms takes courage. The strength to face your fears takes courage. The willingness to risk failure in pursuit of a goal also takes courage.

A woman must develop courage if she is to have even the slightest chance of living a tranquil life. A woman must find courage to live her dreams, courage to live her life with no regrets. A woman who seeks to accomplish anything in life must develop the courage to take calculated risks, to take charge of her life. A woman has to face possible ridicule, confidence shaking criticism, and in some instances sabotage. In the face of all of these things, a woman who is not true to herself, a woman who is afraid to allow her spirit to chart a path to her divine destiny, a woman who dismisses her dreams runs the risk of missing out on opportunities to manifest her true potential.

Working to develop more courage is something that a woman must focus on daily. Indeed, it is through greater courage that a woman is able to achieve inner peace, to ultimately find herself; to finally experience true contentment.

Try some of these seven strategies as you work to increase your courage; tailor them to meet your particular needs, and watch how your personal courage takes you to places that you never thought you'd go. Witness how your personal courage expands your gifts and talents into a phenomenal treasure chest enabling you to achieve your dreams!!!

- ✓ Develop a deep spiritual consciousness and keep an optimistic attitude. Find ways to refresh, reenergize and renew yourself each day.
- ✓ Stay centered on the present and do not keep looking back on the past. Learn from you past, but do not choose to relive it daily.
- ✓ Embrace your uniqueness and do not be afraid to show it.
- ✓ Take the words failure and can't out of your vocabulary. Only speak words of prosperity, hope, possibility and opportunity.
- ✓ Develop your plan and then work it regardless of temporary setbacks, circumstances and disappointments. Stay focused and centered on your goal, not the challenges you face to get there.
- ✓ Remember that failure paves the way to success. Do not fear it or allow past failures to define your present opportunities. Remember failure is definitely not final; failures are merely signs along the path to achievement.
- ✓ Maintain an "I Can" attitude no matter what you face, because no matter what you can.

Courage and Endurance

Key Six Courage

1. Be Not Discouraged

You must accept that occasional disappointment and potential discouragement will come your way, but you do not have to let these temporary setbacks paralyze you, stifle and cripple you forever. In those times when you feel that you are not progressing toward your goals in any aspect of your seven circles, "*be not discouraged.*"

Discouragement is a state of mind that affects us all sometime during our lives. No matter one's station in life, no matter one's fortune or fame, from time to time everyone experiences discouragement. From time to time, everyone faces an overwhelming moment when giving up appears to be the best solution. When such struggles come your way, stay focused on your ultimate goal, listen to your inner spirit, hold fast to your dreams and "*be not discouraged.*"

Even though moments of discouragement will come, allowing it to take hold of you, to totally consume you is not an option. Discouragement is a dangerous phenomenon that can be contagious; an attitude that can be spread one person to another. Although we can not totally isolate ourselves from family or friends who may be suffering from discouragement, we can make a point of insulating one of our most prized possessions from this epidemic; our spirits.

What is discouragement? Discouragement is loosing the desire and motivation to continue doing something that brings purpose and satisfaction to your life because of fear, past failures, or doubt. When discouragement strikes it quickly leads to confusion, then depression. Next, you find yourself losing sight of your goal and so you become withdrawn. Subsequently, a quiet nagging inner despair consumes you. This can all end up creating feelings of spiritual defeat.

What can cause discouragement?

(1) <u>Becoming fatigued due to a loss of personal strength;</u> weariness can lead to physical, mental, emotional, or spiritual exhaustion; if exhausted it is difficult to be motivated

(2) <u>Becoming frustrated due to a loss of vision;</u> loosing sight of or having no goals can make you feel as though life has no meaning

(3) <u>Becoming filled with unconfident feelings and an attitude of failure;</u> failing to pursue your heartfelt dreams or allowing past failures to control your present actions can make you sad, and

(4) <u>Becoming fearful that security or something you hold dear will be lost;</u> allowing people including yourself to kill your dreams or place uncertainty in your heart can make you give up, ultimately causing you to never claim the personal success that is yours for the taking.

What are some cures for discouragement?

(1) Rest, relax and safeguard your body, mind and spirit;

(2) Reorganize your life and better define your priorities;

(3) Seek ways to reinvigorate your spirit and encourage yourself daily;

(4) Reflect and review daily the progress you are making relative to the achievement of your personal goals;

(5) Combat discouragement whenever it tries to invade your head and your heart by performing a quick assessment of your attitude and by determining just what is causing you to feel so much self-doubt; and

(6) Always remember that each setback you face only teaches and strengthens you, moving you closer to your ultimate goal. Remember too that often what appears to be a setback is in fact just a situation divinely designed to lead you to something even more magnificent than you could have ever imagined.

No matter the storms, the challenges, the bouts of despair that may come your way, remember that each of us has been created with special gifts and talents that were meant to be shared with the world.

Finding the courage to live your dreams, while frightening, can actually turn out to be liberating. When you discover the lifework that you want to pursue, the business you want to start or embrace whatever your dream might be, your life will become much more fulfilling and you will ask yourself, "Why did I wait so long to begin enjoying life fully?"

Granted, it takes courage to reclaim your life after a devastating event robs you of your confidence, chips away at your self-esteem, or fills your mind with self-doubt. Yes, it takes perseverance to reach deep within to find the strength to go on, to try once again when you are afraid that you will not accomplish your goal. Nevertheless, it can be done and you can do it!!!

Choose to live life to the fullest, and strive to truly enjoy each day, moment to moment. Seek to balance the seven circles of your life in a manner that works for you. No matter how difficult this may seem, "*be not discouraged.*" Persistently use your talents to pursue your goals with passion and purpose. Whenever doubt knocks at your door, listen intently to your spirit, calm your fears and press on.

No matter what you face, no matter how much effort it takes, no matter what other people might say, trust the power of your dreams and the urgings of your soul, and "*be not discouraged.*"

Exercise 1

My Gateway to Greater Courage

A Time When I Felt Discouraged	How I Felt Discouraged	Why I Felt This Way	Actions I Can Take To Develop Deeper Courage

2. Boundless

Decide today to become boundless. Decide today that from now on you will live your life full of expectation, anticipation, and manifestation. Decide that beginning today that as much as you like pleasing others, you will also start pleasing yourself. Decide today that you will stop working so hard to keep up appearances, and instead start working to meet your needs. Decide today that you will no longer spend your energy chasing someone else's dream, and that instead you will begin to live your own. Decide today that you will choose to be your own person and you will start living a life that feels right for you. Decide to free yourself of the inner turmoil that gnaws at your spirit, as well as the outer chaos that colors your world. Choose to live boundless by opening yourself up to the wonderful possibilities and exciting directions that your life can take.

Becoming boundless takes courage. Becoming boundless requires some calculated risk. Each of us probably knows a woman who decided to live an authentic life. Every woman knows at least one woman who walked out on faith with her life-changing plan in hand. Maybe you know a woman who turned down a promotion to have more time with her family, walked away from a steady income to start up a new business, or left an unhappy marriage in the face of painful disapproval from friends and family. Perhaps you know a woman who started a family after forty, completed her high school diploma in midlife, or took early retirement in order to work full-time as a volunteer.

When you choose to become boundless, you create a life for yourself in which the decisions you make and the actions you take are after sincere consideration, much deliberation, and fully in harmony with what's important to you. When a woman decides to live boundless, the life she chooses my not be the life that others think is right for her, but it is a life that completely fulfills the needs of that woman's heart. At first, the chosen life might even be a little uncomfortable for the woman herself. However, more and more as she greets the day with uncontainable enthusiasm and joy, and goes to bed and sleeps peacefully because of deep personal satisfaction, that woman then knows that she is living her divine life.

Choosing to lift the chains off of your mind and the shackles from around your life takes courage. It takes being honest with yourself and others about who you really are and what you really need to feel personally fulfilled. Becoming boundless begins on the inside before being reflected on the outside.

Determine if you need to make some life changes; ask yourself if any of these statements apply:

- I am skilled and successful in my career, but I am not doing what I love
- I don't know what I want at this moment, but I do know that it is not the life I am currently leading
- I want close relationships, but I escape developing them because of fear or other emotional issues
- I want more personal joy in my life, but I make excuses about making changes right now
- I have dreams and goals that I want to accomplish, but I have not begun to pursue them

Becoming boundless will be a different process for each of us. Becoming boundless will require that every woman travel her own unique path to "self." Whatever the road you must take to begin living more fully, it is sure to be worth the effort.

Your possibilities and your potential are vast. Once you realize that, becoming boundless will become a breeze.

Try some of these strategies as you create your roadmap to self; find the strategy that works best as you develop the courage to be you.

- CELEBRATE YOU. You have been blessed with certain talents and gifts; recognize them, nurture and use them, appreciate them.
- TRY MEDITATION. Find a quiet place and let your inner spirit talk to you; think about the things you would do if failure weren't a possibility.
- FACE YOUR FEARS. Allow yourself to confront your fears about a decision or a plan. Write down exactly what you fear and why.
- FIND THE ROOT CAUSE OF YOUR FEELINGS. Ask yourself, whose voice am I hearing? Who is making me afraid? Is it my voice? My parents? My mother? My sister? The voice of mass media or societal expectations? Friends? Peers?
- LEARN TO MANAGE AROUND THE FEAR. Jot down specific actions you can take to overcome your fears. Move forward productively in spite of them.
- KICK SELF-DOUBT TO THE CURB. Work to complete something that you have been putting off, or work to set one small goal and accomplish it. Small successes can erase self-doubt.

- IDENTIFY A THIRD SOLUTION. Do not agonize over two choices, find a third. This expands your thinking and your opportunities for success.
- DO NOT STRUGGLE WITH THINGS. What is yours is yours, and with sustained effort you will get it, solve it, whatever the case may be. Persist with purpose and know when to let go and allow the Creator to handle things.
- ENJOY THE MOMENT. Immerse yourself in the beauty and pleasure of nature and in daily living. Spend time with people who support, love and appreciate you. Learn to relax and renew daily.
- COMMIT TO YOUR BELIEFS AND DO NOT WAVER. You will feel much better when you stay true to your values and your beliefs.
- DO WHAT YOU CAN. Use your time and your energy wisely. Do not try to please people all of the time because you can't.

3. Confronting Fear

Most women, as do people in general, suffer from five primary fears: a fear of poverty, a fear of death, a fear of failure, a fear of rejection, and a fear brought on by uncertainty or the unknown. While fear is nothing more than *false expectations appearing real*, fear is an emotion that is in our spirit as a protective mechanism. The key becomes to understand that fact and to learn how to put fear in its proper perspective.

The emotion of fear cannot be totally overcome, but it can be confronted and managed. As a woman develops greater courage and awareness, she too becomes better able to confront and face her deepest fears.

There are three insights about fear that a woman must grasp to tackle her fears. The first one is that everyone is afraid. If a person says that they are not afraid, they are simply kidding themselves and trying to impress you. Acknowledging and confronting fear is the real display of courage, not feeble attempts to deny it. A woman who moves forward in pursuit of her goals in the face of her fears is a courageous person. *Fear is Normal.*

The second insight is that the more you work to confront your fears, the less power that fear has over you, and the stronger you become. After a very traumatic experience while driving on a bridge, I developed a fear of heights. Consequently, while driving, any time there was the slightest elevation in the road, I could feel myself begin to panic. After a tough conversation with myself, I began working to face this fear. Slowly, some of my anxiety started to subside. Initially, I just tried to ignore what I was feeling. Eventually, I had to face my fear or I was going to turn myself into a nervous wreck, ultimately stressing myself out even more than the discomfort I first felt. *Fear Must Be Confronted.*

The last insight is start to do the thing that you fear over and over again until your comfort level increases, until the thing that you once feared no longer holds any power over you.

Gaining an understanding of the factors contributing to a fear is a necessary starting point. Many of our fears originate from our childhood conditioning, and we carry these deep-seated beliefs into our adult experiences. Whatever the root cause of a fear, fears left unchecked can paralyze and hold us back from taking positive actions in support of our goals, our dreams, our journey to self. *Fear Can Be Overcome.*

Fear is often caused by lack of information, whether incorrect or incomplete. In some instances, the fear is just based upon a nagging feeling. Our fears tend to lessen when we feel that we are knowledgeable and entirely capable of handling a situation. Our fears are less dominant when we feel healthy and happy. Illness and fatigue can serve to breed fear because our thoughts are not entirely clear.

As soon as a woman realizes that inner peace and a future filled with possibility belongs to risk takers, not security seekers, she is able to create the live she chooses. It should be noted that a woman's life is perverse in the sense that, the more she seeks security, the less of it she actually has. While, the more she seeks opportunity, the more likely she will achieve all of the security that she desires.

Confronting your fears takes courage, day by day. Courage that enables you to face risk, step out on faith and launch your project, or do the thing that is filling your heart with desire. The more you plan and prepare, the more your fear of failure will be silenced. You will grow to see that the confrontation of fears will foster your courage to endure and persist. Persistence is indeed courageous patience because a woman must demonstrate confidence in the choice she has made while waiting to see what the outcome of that choice will bring. When you find yourself becoming full of doubt, refocus your attention on your ultimate goal. Concentrate on the joy you will feel once you accomplish it.

Fear confrontation will also help you to effectively conquer worry. Worry is an example of negative goal setting. When a woman worries she is talking about, thinking about, and imagining all of the things that she does not want to happen. Since we too often get what we expect, too much time spent worrying can end up becoming a self-fulfilling prophecy. In the end, often what a woman fears most comes to fruition. Even when the thing that a woman worries about does not happen, the mental and physical stress that she has brought on herself leaves it mark. To combat worry, try to remain focused on the purposeful actions that you have determined able to achieve your goal. Since our conscious minds can only handle one thought at a time, if you are focused on taking action to achieve your goal, you will not be able to worry about things that could possibly go wrong.

Mastering fear and developing courage are two ingredients to having a happy and contented life. By committing to develop greater courage, you will soon reach a point where fears no longer play a major role in your life or in the decisions that you make. You will feel comfortable embracing your potential and you will be more confident in your ability to achieve them. You will learn to face every situation that comes your way with a sense of calm because of your ability to confront your fears.

Begin by listing in Exercise 2 all of the things that cause you to feel anxious and afraid. Be honest with yourself. You do not have to show this list to anyone. This identification of your fears is for you.

Exercise 2

My Fear Issues

MY FEAR	WHY I AM AFRAID

Exercise 3   Analyzing My Fear Factor

Review the list you prepared in Exercise 2. What are you top two fears? Circle them below, and then use them to complete Exercise 3. This self-reflection should help you better identify possible fears that could be holding you back.

My Top Two Fears
FEAR OF POVERTY
FEAR OF DEATH
FEAR OF FAILURE
FEAR OF REJECTION
FEAR OF UNCERTAINTY

A Specific Time When One Of The Fears Circled Above Held You Back	How Does This Fear Hold You Back In Life	How Does This Fear Help You, or How Has This Fear Helped You In The Past	What Would You Gain By Getting Rid of This Fear	What Actions Can You Take To Overcome This Fear

4. Present…Moment to Moment

Where are you? When your name is called are you staring into the past or gazing into the future? Are you reliving your past on a daily basis, or are you dreaming about and banking on what the future may bring? I challenge you to take a look at your life and ask yourself the question, "Am I Present?"

Learning to live "in the present" is far more difficult than one may realize. Learning to enjoy the life that you have today, learning to be grateful for what you have, and learning to enjoy the gift of life one day at a time are things that escape far too many women. Some of us have gotten into such stifling patterns in our lives that we no longer realize that we are literally hovering out of bounds. Some of us have one or both feet in the past, one foot in the past and another in the future. Some of us have our feet rooted somewhere in the future just waiting for a new day to dawn. How many of us can honestly say that we are fully living in the present?

When you sit quietly thinking, do you spend all of your time wondering how events or relationships would have turned out if you had made different choices? Do you still grapple with anger, guilt or past hurts? Do you still find it difficult to forgive people who have hurt or wronged you? Or do you obsess about past situations trying to uncover ways to have those same experiences again and again?

Don't get me wrong learning from the past is a good thing, as is planning for the future. But if all of your time is spent focused on the past and the future, what are you doing to enjoy life and pursue your goals right now, this present moment.

It is so easy to allow past hurts, disappointment and the wrongs that people have done to us control our lives and our actions. The person can be long gone, the event long past and still we have not let it go and moved on with our lives. Carrying baggage from relationships and love gone bad plagues far too many present-day relationships, eventually causing them to crash and burn. Often, the wounds from our childhood and youthful days have not been soothed. Often, we have not sought spiritual healing. Instead, these remaining scars fester seeping into a woman's present and then on into her future.

When we refuse to live life in the present, we are not allowing change to enter into our lives. When we do not live in the present, it is difficult for us to appreciate all of the goodness that is being bestowed upon us. It is even more difficult for us to embrace the opportunities that are knocking at our door, beckoning us to develop our gifts and talents in service to others and for our own personal fulfillment.

The past is gone and you cannot change it. The only thing that the past can do for you is provide you with life lessons that can help you to live better in the present and even more joyfully in the future. When we dwell in the past we almost become like a programmed robot, repeating the same actions, choices and behaviors over and over again. Why? We have not left our past and shifted into the present. When we feel guilt, it is because we are focused on the past. When we feel fear, it is because we are focused on the future. Both of these mental situations do nothing but drain us and cause us a tremendous amount of unneeded stress. This way of thinking is truly a waste of our energy because in the final analysis all we have right now is this present moment.

When you live in the present you are fully aware of all of the things you are thinking, feeling and doing. By being present you are seeing things and people as they are and you are not allowing your present to be dominated by your past or how someone use to be. Being present means that fear, anger, disappointment, hurt or even past success are not clouding your view of things today. Two people can experience the same event but have totally different perceptions. This is due in part because of the amount of emotional and spiritual baggage that the person is still carrying around with them.

Strive to live "in the present" and enjoy your life today. Work to bring closure to past events and old hurts. Move to end negative relationships that do nothing but assault your spirit and damage your personal well-being. Being totally present in the moment can help a woman immerse herself in joy, creativity, and the pursuit of her dreams. Fully enjoying the present enables a woman to benefit from the current opportunities flowing her way

When you find yourself dwelling in the past, gently nudge yourself and then ask the question, "Am I present?" Quickly get in touch with what you are really feeling and uncover your concerns. Address them and encourage yourself to deal with the right now. Then ease yourself gently on back into the moment. Sister, enjoy your present because in the end that is all that you have.

5. The "Ah Ha" Moment

One of these days, hopefully sooner that later, your "ah ha" moment will come. In an unexpected flash, a life-changing situation will come your way, and the realizations that a woman derives from this occurrence can serve to strengthen her. The question will be does the woman have the courage to recognize it, accept it, and face up to what this special moment in time is trying to teach her.

Just as inspiration is something that comes in waves, a woman's "ah ha" moment will feel as though a powerful starlight has been switched on inside of her. A woman's "ah ha" moment comes when she has opened her mind and her heart to possibility, to opportunity, to new ways of doing something. Every women's "ah ha" moment will be unique and special, just as extraordinary as the woman is in all of her glory. Your "ah ha" moment may come through your solving a personal problem of your own or for a friend, perhaps finally finding the answer to a question that has been troubling you for quite sometime, or perhaps finding a way to address a challenge that has been facing you. Be on the lookout for your "ah ha" moments so that you can experience their wonderment and relish the good feeling for days to come.

Your "ah ha" moments will lead you to a level of deeper understanding and greater inner peace. Reaching your "ah ha" moment may require persistence and commitment because it may take some pondering on your part to arrive at a point of knowing what your spirit desires. To achieve a life that fills you with contentment, you must be courageous enough to toil away searching until you find the answer. If you are feeling tired, sad or as though something is missing in your life, perhaps this is because your energy is drained as you refuse to acknowledge your "ah ha" moments. Pushing these life lessons to the rear of your awareness can only make you feel like a pressure cooker that has built up way too much steam. No matter how hard you may try, if your heart and spirit are not in it, you will not feel much personal passion for the life path you are currently traveling. You must be willing to give yourself a chance to be who you truly are. Your "ah ha" moments will help you find your center; find the woman within.

An "ah ha" moment will cause a woman to choose one of three attitudes. She will become like a carrot, an egg, or a coffee bean. If she becomes a carrot, whenever challenges that cause pressure come her way, a carrot woman softens, and become ineffective. Much like overcooked carrots in a pot of hot water, women who are carrots find it extremely difficult to function when things get tough. Women who are eggs appear able to handle the heat of "ah ha" moments with little difficulty and they typically seem to accomplish these feats with not much effort. The only problem with women who are eggs is that while they do not crack under such pressure, they become hardened on the inside. This harsh interior makes many women become cold, calculating, unloving and insensitive. Women who are like coffee beans become stronger, better, more effective as a result of their life lessons and "ah ha" moments. Just as the fragrance, potency and full flavor of a coffee bean is unleashed in hot water, coffee bean women just seem to get better with time.

The answer may come when you least expect it and this is what makes the "ah ha" moment even more spectacular. Instead of chasing, fighting and forcing an answer to come, open up your inner being, relax and trust your spirit knowing that it will give you the answers that you seek. For you see, all of the answers, all of a women's solutions to everything can be found inside of her, if she is ready to listen. Are you ready to listen to your "ah ha moments?

A Woman Who Is Missing Her "Ah Ha" Moments	A Woman Who Listens For Her "Ah Ha" Moments
She feels anxious a lot of the time	She feels optimistic and capable
She tries to be a people-pleaser	She is able to think for herself
She second guesses every decision	She trusts her judgment and always just tries to do her best
She is very rigid	She can accept change
She rationalizes her actions	She takes responsibility for her actions
She tries to impress others	She is honest and open with others; she is true to herself
She says and does things she regrets	She knows when to apologize and she does
She has low expectations	She has high expectations and expects to be successful
She suffers from a victim attitude	She is nobody's victim; she gives and demands respect
She hides her feelings a great deal of the time	She is able to express her feelings
She is stifled by fear or disappointment	She faces her fears and works through them
She feels helpless or hopeless	She does not suffer from learned hopelessness, she chooses optimism
She suffers from addictive behavior	She works on improving herself daily
She is depressed or extremely angry	She is joyous and free of past anger
She has lost sight of her dreams	She is pursuing her dreams with vigor
She tries to always smooth things over	She speaks her opinion in a constructive manner
She has no goals	She has goals and a plan to achieve them
She listens intently to her inner critic	She minimizes her negative self-talk
She feels overwhelmed and confused	She is focused and self-confident
She repeats the same behaviors	She develops good habits and works to halt negative ones
She maintains negative relationships	She forms nurturing and mutually supportive relationships

6. Finding Courage To Be You

Courage comes in all forms and in a variety of fashions; for courage is overcoming your fear of something, and forcing yourself to try to do the very thing that causes a great deal of trepidation.

We have all come face to face with a moment in time, an activity or a task that provoked strong feelings of inner turmoil, discomfort and strife. At that precise moment, we had to make a decision. Will I give into my fear or will I force myself to grow; will I seek to expand my personal experiences?

It can take courage to sing that solo at church, or make that presentation at work. It can take courage to share your honest feeling with a family member, a friend or your mate. It can take courage to go to the doctor when you suspect that you are not well. It can take courage to acknowledge your own personal truths. It can take courage to hop onto an amusement park ride, or to change a habit that is stifling your personal growth. For some people, after a failed relationship, it can take courage to get involved with someone else again.

Courage can be an extremely allusive thing, because often one experience, an attitude, or a personal belief can stand in the way of our pursuit of the things that we want.

We all harbor our dreams deep with our souls. Sometime we reflect on our dreams and for a few minutes we allow ourselves to think about how things can be. On other occasions, we keep them tucked away so that our dreams cannot intrude on what we are doing. After all, we are simply too busy living life to be inconvenienced by our dreams. When that is the case, clearly we have not yet learned that until we follow the urging of our hearts, we will be filled with discontent and longing in our souls.

Finding the courage to live your dreams, while frightening, can actually turn out to bring a considerable amount of contentment. You only get one life, so why not choose to spend it happily doing the things that you enjoy. Be courageous and persist until you achieve your aim. Follow your heart and listen to your soul. You owe it to yourself to use the talents divinely bestowed upon you, so that you can become the person you were destined to become. Decide to discover yourself, and then choose to become the real you.

7. Sister, Do The Dash

If you stop to think about it, the reality of the human experience is that from the moment of our birth, we begin a journey in preparation for eternal life. We relate in this world through several different methods: spiritual, through our souls, and our emotions. Our spirits relate to the spiritual realm relating to the things above us; this is our belief and relationship with the Creator. The soul relates to the things around us, family, the environment, friends, love ones, our work and personal lives. The emotional experience is comprised of our belief system, our thoughts, our reactions to things inside of us, and how our feelings serve to color our visions of the world.

One of the most prized possessions we are given as a part of this our human experience is the gift of time. Time is the vehicle through which we manifest our potential. Now what we do with this gift of time is another story. A person's time can be spent productively doing things that help them to grow and experience life fully, or a non-productive focus can lead to negativity, anger and lost dreams. A woman's productive use of her time goes a long way to help her live the life of her dreams. This is true because the personal harvest that a woman is able to reap reflects how she has used her time.

We all start out with that all-important date, the day that we are born. This is a time when our minds and creativity are still very clear and un-tampered with. Life is still experienced with wonderment. When we pass on, our friends and loved ones poignantly remember the date that we go home to the Creator. This is a time when people reflect on how we lived and how we impacted the lives of others. So there you have it, two pivotal dates that document our time on the planet. More critical than both of these dates is what a woman does with the time in between.

On your tombstone, as much as no one wants to dwell on this evitable day, etched in the stone will be both of these dates, birth and death. Nestled in between will be a small dash. While it may not be that large of a dash, that dash will say a lot about you. In a sense, your dash will serve to define you. It is in that dash that you will be remembered. With that in mind, it brings me to the question that I ask myself daily, and you should probably be asking yourself this question too, "What am I doing with my dash?"

Using the life that you have been given is something that should be directing your steps. Using each day to bring joy and fulfillment to yourself and others is an attitude that should dominant everything that you do. Choosing to use the life that you have been given to do more than just make a living is up to you. Choosing instead to make a difference in this world is a choice that every woman will have to make. No woman knows when her earthly experience will end, so she owes it to herself to use every precious moment chasing after her dreams, doing the things that she enjoys, enjoying relationships with others, becoming the person that she was intended to be.

If you are not living your life according to your values, aspirations, dreams and intentions, then sister you are not doing the dash. If you are living your life today under the clouds of past disappointment, pain and sadness, sister you are not doing the dash. How you use your dash is entirely up to you. But know that a life worth leading is a life to be remembered. So come on sister, get courageous and do the dash. Put on your magic slippers each and every day and do the dash. Live with a sense of purpose and enjoy your own fantastic carpet ride each and every day. Do the dash sister girl and do it in style, yours.

The Alphabet for Women Who Live Soulfully

A is for aspire	You thirst to become the woman you were meant to be; your dreams lead you steps and quench your soul; you are constantly striving for more
B is for belief	You know that you can accomplish whatever you put your mind to pursue; your know what you deserve
C is consciousness	You are fully aware of your choices and opportunities; you are fully engaged in your life
D is for dedication	You are committed to yourself and others
E is for effort	You put your full energy and time into the things you pursue; you give your all always
F is for faith	You know that the Creator is there for you in good times and bad; you know that you will prevail
G is for gratitude	You appreciate the things that you already have and know that through your faith and belief more goodness is on the way
H is for hope	You approach life filled with anticipation and optimism, you have optimistic perspectives everyday
I is for intention	You make choices and live your life based upon your values, your goals, your dreams
J is for joy	You give and get delight from life each day
K is for kindness	You are warm and gentle to others
L is for love	You give unconditional love and support to others
M is for meaningful	You appreciate and enjoy the experiences in your life
N is for nurture	You nurture yourself therefore you are able to nurture others
O is for opportunity	You know that the chances for you to live your dreams come each day
P is for purpose	You use your gifts and talents for a reason; you are guided by goals
Q is for quest	You seek to be and do all that your potential will allow
R is for resilience	You do not allow the storms of life to derail you, you fall down but you get right back up and try again
S is for serenity	You understand the importance of inner peace and you seek it
T is for tenacity	You do not know the meaning of quit, and I Can't is not in your vocabulary
U is for unstoppable	You refuse to give in or give up; you are determined
V is for value	You are guided by your values and your spirit
W is for warmhearted	You are a joy to know and to love; you leave your mark everywhere
X is for eXhilirate	You encourage others to become their best
Y is for yearn	You know that you must honor your spirit and your soul, you have a deep desire to live your calling
Z is for zeal	You have an enthusiasm for life and living, and it shows

My road to greater courage has been growing slowly. Through personal challenges, life situations, various obstacles and my interactions with family, friends, and even my husband, I have gained a deeper level of courage. For as long as I can remember, I always sought to fit in. I allowed a host of feelings and emotions to keep me from showing others my authentic self. I can still remember clearly while growing up that I did a lot of things that I really did not want to do because I wanted to fit in with my peers. On numerous occasions, I let my actions be guided by the dictates of others, fearful that if I acted differently I would be ostracized.

Through greater courage, I now understand that being different, accepting yourself and marching to your own style of music is certainly all right. My journeys have shown me that there are other people who share my viewpoints and have similar aspirations. I now realize that these are the people who should form my inner circle, not people who demand that I become a carbon copy.

A woman has to develop a sense of courage to handle the relationships, situations, choices and circumstances in her life. The sooner a woman decides to truly be herself, the better her life will become. People will learn to accept you and love you for the person that you are, and those people that can not appreciate you, are probably not people that you should interacting with anyway. A woman cannot live a fulfilling and joyful life until she develops the courage to stand alone in situations or be willing to fly solo as it relates to her choices. She certainly will not be able to discover and develop her true calling or a vision for her life if she does not begin with a strong fundamental understanding of herself, or have the courage to exhibit it.

Courage is an important characteristic for a woman to possess. For in those moments when continuing a course of action, or making a difficult decision, or rebounding after a disappoint, without measures of courage a woman will want to quit and just let matters be. Without courage, a woman will simply give up and quietly put her hopes, dreams and aspirations on a back burner. Finding the personal strength to keep trying when one part of your being keeps saying give it up takes deep conviction and courage. Every woman has the capacity to develop that level of courage by simply deciding to become unstoppable.

Strengthen your depth of courage each day by identifying your fears and facing them; by defining your dreams and following them; by resolving all issues and challenges you encounter and persisting with your life vision. With fountains of courage, a woman can withstand the storms of life when they come. Through developing her courage, a woman will grow stronger day by day.

Pearls of Wisdom for Soulful Living—Courage

Courage is the strength to go on in the face of gut wrenching fear.

A woman with courage is willing to be herself, love herself, seek her dreams, and never give up ever.

Without courage, you will never be YOU.

Be not discouraged, for if you pursue your passions with intent, purpose and dogged persistence,
you cannot fail.

Courage is continuing in pursuit of your dream, your choice, and your aim even when you are filled with moments of doubt, flurries of criticism, and the comments of naysayers.

Resiliency

THE SEVENTH KEY TO SOULFUL LIVING

How do you see yourself, as a victim or survivor, or are you a thrivor? Have you been able to bounce back after a major disappointment? Have you been able to recover from a failed relationship, an unsuccessful project, or a lost job or business? Have you been able to reframe the negative mental scripts learned during childhood or in the midst of abusive environments? How about mending your broken heart because unloving parents crushed it, from a painful experience in a foster care system, or from living with extended family that did not really want you and they let you know it every opportunity that they got? How about surviving a messy divorce? What about recovering from the scare of cancer, the death of a loved one, or pressing on in the face of one setback after another?

When you think about an ability to recover from any of these occurrences, I am not talking about simply crippling along. I am talking about having the ability to heal emotional, physical, and spiritual wounds fully; being able to fully participate in life once again. I am talking about bringing closure to the events of days gone by, and moving on with your life learning valuable lessons from these events. I am thinking of an ability to use this knowledge to become a woman of substance, a woman of faith, courage and personal strength. I am talking about a woman who does not dwell on the events and details from her past, but instead a woman who uses this information to create a strong future for herself.

I dare say few women possess that ability all of the time without a second thought. But if you already do, hats off to you because you are indeed a rare breed. Most women are more like me, working hard to hold on to their sanity and their senses as they work to overcome life's inevitable obstacles. Most women are trying desperately to make positive changes in their lives, trying to let go of ill will, bad feelings, hurt and pain. Most women are fighting with themselves as they attempt to let go of self-blame, self-doubt and self-anger because of choices and decisions that they wish could be reversed. By changing your beliefs and your attitude, a woman can free herself from those psychological and emotional chains that may be making it difficult for her to progress forward. Indisputably, a change in a woman's mindset can unlock her innate ability to desire and achieve success.

I have maintained my ability to love even though my heart has been broken countless times because of obvious bad choices in men. I hold on to an attitude of optimism even though I have made so many foolish and reckless decisions in both my work and personal lives. I have overcome the disappointment of a failed marriage when my mate decided he loved crack cocaine more than most anything. I have rebounded from an unsuccessful business and went on to complete my doctorate. I have been able to weather many a setback and still believe that my possibilities and opportunities to prevail were still plentiful. This attribute is a powerful force for a woman to possess. I am talking about the notion of resiliency, and the more of it you have, the farther you can travel in this uncertain world.

Resiliency is the ability to effectively manage your stress. Resiliency is the ability to deal with and be flexible in the rapidly changing global world in which we live, being able to deal with the life changes that come our way. Resiliency is your capacity to face this ebb and flow of stress and change and be able to bounce back extremely quickly from setbacks that confront you. If you are resilient, you are able to master the art of flowing with life instead of fighting, struggling against it.

The power of resiliency is inside every woman, but she must learn how to tap into it so that she can prevent, minimize and in some cases overcome the sometime potentially damaging effects of life's adversities. Being resilient means that a woman is able to tap into her innermost strengths in order to adapt. A resilient woman continues to develop in a positive fashion, even in the face of life's negative experiences. The more resilient a woman is, the more confident she becomes about her abilities to deal with change, challenge and adversity.

A resilient woman understands that her inner powers can sustain her, and she remains centered and focused on her abilities to achieve personal success and fulfillment. A resilient woman is in touch with her true self and she refuses to fall prey to the social or false expectations that many women have grown to accept. A resilient woman is able to bring more peace and joy in her life because she withstands both the gentle breezes of a calm sunny morn, and the fierce harsh winds of a turbulent stormy day. A resilient woman is able to flourish, no matter the weather, no matter the season. Resilient women refuse to be denied because they are determined to succeed.

Key Seven Resiliency

1. The Resiliency Factor

There has been a great deal of research and much written about the resiliency factor. Research has uncovered the fact that resiliency occurs naturally in all of us but every woman's ability to recognize and tap into it varies tremendously. Sadly, some women are not able to use their resiliency factor at all.

Finding a way to enhance your mental, emotional and spiritual capacities is possible if a woman develops stronger connections with her true inner power and natural gifts. The clearer a woman's goals are in her mind the easier it becomes for her to rebound from life's setbacks. With defined goals, a woman is able to overcome any challenges that she might face. Your resiliency factor is intricately tied to your beliefs and your attitudes. A woman's beliefs and attitudes are important building blocks when it comes to the level of her resiliency. A woman's beliefs and attitudes say much about how she thinks and feels about herself. If a woman thinks that she can overcome any obstacle that she faces, she can. But if a woman's spirit and mind feel defeated, her ability to bounce back from inevitable change and life's adversities is limited.

Developing your ability to rebound requires that a woman learn to understand the relationship between her thoughts, feelings and behaviors. A woman must uncover what she says to herself whenever she is faced with an obstacle, and know how these thoughts control her actions. A woman must learn to overcome her limiting beliefs so that they do not hinder her over and over again. Finding ways to deal with and relieve stress enhances a woman's ability to develop a resilient mindset because she knows how to make her thoughts and moods more harmonious.

A woman who is living soulfully, and is working to bring more joy and inner peace into her life should focus on strengthening her personal attributes and confidence in the following areas:

- ❖ The Power of Your Mind—create a positive belief system and an attitude of optimism so that you are able to see yourself succeeding and know you have the ability to act upon your goals
- ❖ The Power of Emotional Intelligence—broaden your knowledge and personal discipline in support of healthy emotional, mental and social awareness; know how your emotions affect your choices and behavior

- ❖ The Power of Relationships—build and maintain healthy and supportive interpersonal relationships, set standards for your relationships and stick to them consistently; unhealthy relationships only hinder you
- ❖ The Power of Learning—appreciate life-long learning, embrace change, and be willing to recognize and develop your talents
- ❖ The Power of Values—embrace values and principles that form the foundation of your life; your values should enable you to live with respect, resilience, righteousness and responsibility
- ❖ The Power of Vision—know the importance of creating a vision for your life, developing goals and a plan of action to accomplish that vision
- ❖ The Power of Example—serve as a role model by exhibiting the power of courage, commitment, compassion and learned wisdom

A woman with high levels of resiliency has personal insight, and is able to communicate her true feelings when questioning others or when being asked for answers; she is independent and only maintains healthy supportive relationships; she demonstrates initiative and proactively solves her problems; she exhibits her creativity and her sense of humor; and her personal values serve as the building blocks for her actions.

A resilient woman knows that a temporary obstacle does not have to be a permanent roadblock. A resilient woman knows that she must set her course, navigate the sometime turbulent waters, and remain focused on her destination.

Exercise 1 — Personal Power

Think about the personal power that you possess. Think about the strengths that you already have and detail how you are using these personal strengths to help you accomplish your goals and improve the quality of your life each day. For those strengths you seek to develop, write down how you will use them as you continue to develop your personal power over time.

Sister, You Got the Power!!!!!!!!!!!!!

The Power	How I Already or Will Use It
Self	
Vision	
Attitude	
Habits	
Values	
Conscious Living	
Spirit	
Religion	
Choice	
Love	
Supportive Relationships	
Forgiveness	
Gratitude	
Effort	
Time	
Thought	
Creativity	
Hope	
Belief	
Change	
Experience	
Success	
Resiliency	
Inner Peace	
Purpose	
Passion	
You Fill In Blank_____	
You Fill In Blank_____	
You Fill In Blank_____	
You Fill In Blank_____	
You Fill In Blank_____	
You Fill In Blank_____	

Exercise 2 How Resilient Are You??

Honestly Rate How Much Each Of The Following Apply To You. Place A Check Mark In The Box of The Rating That Best Describes Your Level of Resiliency.

1–Very Little   5–Very Much
Total Your Personal Rating By Adding Up The Scores For Your Responses

My Ratings

	1	2	3	4	5
I am curious, ask questions, want to know how things work, I experiment					
I constantly learn from my experiences and the experiences of others					
I need and expect things to work well for me and others, I care for myself					
I handle new developments, find humor in things and I am able to laugh at myself					
I adapt quickly to change, I am highly flexible					
I feel comfortable and accept conflicting qualities in myself					
I anticipate problems and avoid conflicts					
I develop improved self-esteem and self-confidence every year					
I listen and read others well, I am able to deal with difficult people with empathy					
I manage the emotional side of adversity and I am able to recover; I grieve, honor and am able to let the past go					
I expect tough situations to work out well; I am able to press on in the face of obstacles, I am able to help others and bring stability in times of uncertainty and turmoil					
I find the gift in accidents and bad experiences					
I am able to convert misfortune into good fortune					
I think up creative solutions to challenges, I invent ways to solve problems, I trust intuition and hunches					

MY TOTAL _____

If you score 60-70, you are HIGHLY RESILIENT, you are better than most
If you score 40-50, you are ADEQUATE
If you score 30-40, you are STRUGGLING
If you score under 30, you should SEEK HELP or WORK ON BECOMING MORE RESILIENT

2. Begin Again and Again

How many times in conversations with family, friends, even in mental conversations that you have with yourself, have you uttered the words, "If only I could have a second chance". Do you ever feel like you have wasted some of your valuable opportunities, or that you have made some truly bad decisions and just can't seem to forgive yourself? Have you ever felt regrouping and redefining your life is impossible? Do you feel as though you have simply blown a relationship, a dream, or a personal goal?

Stop for a moment and think about what you are claiming as your own personal truths. Ask yourself what beliefs you have that make you think that you only get "one turn" at love, at opportunity, at life. This could not be further from the truth and as soon as you understand this, the more rewarding your life will become. The fact of the matter is that your chances to successfully accomplish a goal do not end until you decide to give up. The reality of this life is that you can begin again and again. You can have a second chance, a third even a fourth.

Far too many women let the past hold them back. Broken hearts, broken promises, past mistakes, and past failures too often dominate some of our thoughts. Letting go and moving on is difficult but necessary if a woman is really going to enjoy today, the present. Straddling the fence between the past and the present is difficult, not to mention draining. A woman must vow to leave the past where it belongs, way back there. Learn from it, grow from it, but refuse to dwell and wallow in it.

Do not allow the dreaded dirty dozen to block you way: I had no choice; I had no control; I don't know; I forgot; I'll try; I will wait until something happens, then I will do something; Nobody told me; It's not my fault; It's not my job; I Can't; That's just the way I am; I'll wait and see.

A chance is a likelihood that something will happen, a real opportunity to make something happen. A woman's chance to make a life change, a career change; a personal change is what she believes it to be; for the extent of our effort and our level of persistence depends on what we think we deserve and how hard we are willing to work to get it.

Now when I find myself focused entirely too much on my past mistakes, find myself filled with a nagging uncertainty that my chances of accomplishing my goal is small, I ask myself "What would you do if failure was not even a possibility?" My response is always to forge ahead, to go for it, and with that I begin again.

3. Everything Must Change

Accepting the change in something that you enjoy, something that you feel comfortable with, or something that you have grown to know is often difficult. One aspect of being resilient is how well a woman is able to accept and adapt to change. Everything changes; nothing stays the same, that's just the way things go. A woman who uses her energy to embrace change as it occurs, instead of fighting it, is better able to continue moving forward rather than becoming paralyzed.

Mind you, I am not saying that all change is good; what I am saying is that change is change, and the vast majority of change cannot be stopped. This leads a woman to two possible choices, either she can adjust to the change and flourish, or refuse to accept the change and languish in a sea of complaints.

Change can be terribly uncomfortable, change can be unnerving, and change may require you to alter your plans. But no matter what changes you face, you have the power to handle it. Why? Because you hold that power in your mind and in your heart.

I had to learn this lesson the hard way. When a hurricane devastated the Virgin Islands, my husband thought it best if we moved to the US for a while to regroup. Reluctantly, I agreed. We packed up the few possessions that had weathered the storm and relocated.

From the moment I arrived, I felt like a fish out of water. I missed the beauty of my favorite beaches and the sounds of St. Thomas. I struggled through each day trying to hold my head up high and not burst into tears because of my personal despair. In retrospect, although I had verbally agreed to the move, my heart and mind was not in it. I fought the change for a long, long while. I fought the change until I got tired of fighting it. Finally, I changed my frame of mind and chose to start being grateful that I had survived the hurricane and had landed a job that I thoroughly enjoyed. I treasured spending more time with my parents. The more I opened myself up to accept the change, the more new opportunities knocked on my door. Surprisingly, I became more content.

Now, I realize that my fighting the change for so long actually blocked my progress. Now, I understand that without the change a number of the opportunities for personal growth that I have been given would not have occurred if we had not left St. Thomas. I now know that it is necessary to look at change as a vessel to expanded opportunities and a preparatory school for the next good thing that is trying to make its way into your life. I now know that just as one change occurs so will another. When the time is right, another change will come again. I even know that when the time is right, I will return to my life in the Caribbean.

When change comes into your life, be open to accepting it with your mind and your spirit. When change comes, open your eyes to the opportunities that it offers. You see my dear sister, in the end, you just might like where it takes you.

4. Pursue the Opportunity in the Obstacle

Centered in the midst of every dark cloud is a rainbow waiting to reveal itself. You may not see it right away, but the longer and more closely you look, the more evident that rainbow becomes. The relationship between obstacles and opportunity is very much the same, particularly, if your resiliency factor is pretty strong.

So often, a woman will have a specific plan or goal in mind, and because her acceptance of change does not come easy, she sees any slight deviation from what she has envisioned as a major obstacle. Mind traps can hinder us; mind traps can make it extremely difficult to see the opportunity tucked inside of that small, yet temporary dark cloud.

Common mind traps a woman might have that can hamper her ability to accept change and reap the full benefit of her experiences are:

- ❖ Jumping to Quick Conclusions—you reach a decision before getting all of the facts, you make quick assumptions
- ❖ No Vision, Just Tunnel Vision—you only see things one way or the other, and most of the time your view is negative
- ❖ Just How You See It—you tend to magnify the negatives in your life and minimize the positives
- ❖ Everything Is Not About You—you personalize things a great deal and when things go wrong you blame yourself or feel that it must be something that you said or did wrong
- ❖ Take Responsibility When Its Yours—you never accept responsibility for anything, it is always someone else's fault
- ❖ It's All The Same—you generalize about things without first getting all of the facts
- ❖ It's A Mind Thing—you can not read people's minds, so hear people out before you make a decision
- ❖ Emotional Intelligence—you make decisions based primarily on your feelings giving little thought to reason

When we face an obstacle, it tends to play out something like this:

The Obstacle—→ Limiting Personal Beliefs/Attitude————→ Responding Emotionally————→ View Obstacle As A Major Problem————→Negative Reaction—→Worry/Stress-→ Decision/Solution Based Upon Emotions and Fear

Instead, what a woman should strive for is something like this:

The Obstacle—→ Strong Personal Beliefs/Attitude————→ Assessing the Situation Rationally—→ Identity Potential Beneficial Aspects Or Learning to Be Gained From The Obstacle————→Acceptance of the Change in the Situation→Calm/Self-confidence response Show of Faith and Persistence In Solving the Obstacle....→Decision/Solution Based Upon Adaptation and Strategy Revision

Sometimes obstacles are necessary in order to force us to come up with a better plan, refine an idea, or to consider factors that may have initially escaped us. Obstacles, though burdensome can make us stronger and actually prepare us for greater challenges yet to come. Obstacles, if we choose to view them in this way, can actually help us to hone our skills in a field of choice, move closer to accomplishment of a goal, or to improve our entrepreneurial business acumen.

A woman must remain focused on what she expects to achieve. She must have the faith to know that no matter what road bumps she encounters her expectations will be her manifestation.

Exercise 3   Interview With An Obstacle

Conduct an open dialogue with one of your toughest obstacles. Allow your most positive inner voice to ask your obstacle the following questions. All you have to do is be the note taker, not a gatekeeper that keeps you from uncovering your mental roadblocks. Sister, let the truth be told.

1. Obstacle, what is your name?

2. Why are you such a challenge for me, why don't you just go away?

3. How have I attempted to overcome you in the past?

4. How have you defeated me and my attempts to overcome you up till now?

5. What personal qualities will I need to defeat you?

6. What different actions will I need to take so that I can conquer you?

7. What different thoughts and emotions will I need to take control of you?

8. What different beliefs will I need to triumph over you?

9. What important lesson have you come to teach me?

10. How can I use this situation to help me grow stronger?

5. Failure is not Final

The vast majority of women let their fear of failure keep them from actively pursuing success. The vast majority of women clings to past failures and relive that devastating event daily in their minds, replaying the event repeatedly in their hearts. Instead of learning from the experience, most women allow a temporary setback we call failure to place fear in their spirits, ultimately making the woman deeply afraid to continue chasing her dreams. A woman's view and ability to deal with failure is critical. For a woman's perspective regarding failure tends to impact every aspect of her life.

As women, we plan for success and we make long lists of things we will do when we succeed, but rarely do we plan for handling failure. Rarely do women prepare mentally for the inevitable obstacles and life challenges that can and will confront us. Of course, no one sets out planning to fail. But the reality of the human experience is that not all of the choices we make will be right for the situations at hand. Nor will all of the roads we decide to take contribute positively to the achievement of a desired goal.

Most women go through life not understanding that failure is only a step in a process that leads to success. Instead of viewing failure as a finality, as a nail in our personal coffins, failure should be viewed as a way to determine what will work, a good way to find answers.

Too often we label isolated events as failures, focusing not on the big picture, but on a single wrong turn taken while making the journey to success. Once we understand that occasional failure is unavoidable; failure is not an event but merely an indicator that you did not consider or master all of the steps needed to achieve your goal; failure is in the eye of the beholder because you ultimately are the one who chooses to label an event as a failure, and failure is not a stigma or the enemy, only then are you truly prepared to unlock the gateway to your personal success and fulfillment.

Most of the people that we view as successful will quickly tell you that everything that led to their success also came from their failures. Hard as it is to accept, there is benefit in every event that occurs in your life.

Women who understand that failure is not the end of world, demonstrate the following abilities: they do not take instances of failure personally and they do not see a failure as determining their self-worth; they realize that failure is only a temporary situation; they see failure as an isolated incident that is not permanent; they have realistic expectations and know that the more a person wants to achieve the stronger their positive mental needs to be; they focus on their strengths and work to enhance their weaknesses; they vary their approaches and they try different things until they find what works; and they are able to rebound after a mistake, failure or error.

Vow to make failure your friend. For through failure, we are able to find success. Remember failure is only a temporary, isolated incident, not a life sentence designed to hold us forever hostage. Ask yourself what it is you want. Then, stare the possibility of failure directly in the face, smile, and with courage go forth and passionately pursue your dreams.

Exercise 4   Facing the Prospect of a Setback

Use this tool to plan ahead for possible setbacks, obstacles and challenges that you might face. They may not come, but if they do, you will be ready.

My Goal	
List the things that could possibly happen	How will you deal with those things should they occur

6. Choose Happiness

No matter what happens to us, no matter how our plans might change, how we respond to these situations is up to each of us. Deciding to move forward with a positive attitude even though you have just been sideswiped by something unexpected is an attitude, a mindset, and more than anything else a choice. Situations and circumstances do not define us; they reveal us. The classroom of life that every woman sits in will be different. Every class, every curriculum, every lesson, and every homework assignment will vary and will be uniquely designed to foster the personal growth and development of that special woman.

A woman's success in this life is not measured by how much she owns, the list of accomplishments that she may pile up on a resume, or the devastating details of her personal predicaments. The true measure of a woman's life is how she has dealt with and overcome the challenges that have come her way; how well she has performed in her own life classroom. Every woman has the capacity to excel in her life classroom, but to do so, she will need and must create inner peace and spiritual harmony. Choosing happiness is a woman's stepping-stone to that level of personal contentment.

Happiness is an exhilarating feeling. When we are happy we feel satisfied, peaceful, grateful, and feel a tremendous degree of affection for ourselves and for others. In our most natural state from birth all we know is joy and contentment. A women's inability to experience this contentment in later life results from learned behaviors that she has grown to accept as a part of life, just the way things are. When a woman realizes that this is truly not the case, she is able to transform her life and her experiences.

How does a woman learn to choose happiness?

- *By understanding the power of thoughts*—much like a woman's beating heart is a part of living, so are her thoughts, the only difference is that although her thoughts are continuous, she has control over what she chooses to believe, what she chooses to make her reality; everything a woman feels first begins as a thought. Three key points to remember: you are the thinker of your thoughts, you need to be perceptive about your relationship with your thoughts, and you do not have to take each and every thought that comes into your mind seriously

- *By understanding her moods*—just like thoughts, changing moods are part of being human; a woman should learn to assess her moods and always try to determine what is causing her to feel that way, learning to keep moods in their proper perspective is a woman's best weapon against allowing temporary setbacks to change her otherwise positive attitude. Three key points to remember: your moods may change from high to low, but these shifts in mood do not change your life; do not take your low moods to heart for they will past; do not make decisions when you are in a low mood, make them when you are in a high mood because you can think more clearly

- *By understanding everybody has a different reality*—the sooner a woman understands that everybody sees things differently, she becomes more open to compromise and less open to conflict. Three key points to remember: you can not change other people only yourself, you can not change the viewpoints of others, only share your own; you are better able to achieve mutual benefit in every situation that comes your way once you understand that every person's reality is unique

- *By understanding your feelings*—a woman's feelings alert her to the extent of internal conflict she is feeling, when your thoughts are predominantly negative and depressing, it is a signal that your belief system is dominating your feelings and negatively impacting your ability to cope; when a woman is in control of her feelings, the facts not her circumstances determine her response

- *By understanding the now*—as difficult as it may be, a woman must find ways to accept, heal, learn and release her past; a woman must learn to live and be present in the "right now", holding on to past disappointments, discouragement and mistakes makes it hard for a woman to see the opportunities that are presently coming her way; bring closure to the past so that you are enjoying today right now, and prepare for even more contentment in the future

Deciding to be happy is a choice and an attitude that you can make your own. It is a matter of wanting happiness in your life and working to maintain it daily through conscience living, attitude monitoring and personal understanding. Decide to choose happiness without fail. Genuine happiness can be yours if you invite it into your heart and embrace it into your soul.

7. Becoming Emotionally Intelligent

A woman's emotional intelligence is her greatest predictor of personal success; not her IQ, not her beauty, not her family history, not how many degrees she may hold.

In the world of work and in life, one's awareness of emotions and how they affect you has been found in government studies and over 15 global company reports to be twice as important as raw intelligence and technical knowledge. While this may be shocking in one fashion, when you stop to think about it, every woman knows someone or perhaps when thinking of yourself, an instance where an inability to understand or manage your emotions made it impossible to handle a situation effectively.

A researcher coined the phrase, emotionally intelligent, or EI in 1995, but the concept has been around since 1920. The world we live in is filled with constant change, and a person's ability to deal with such rapid change hinges on the level of their adaptability, resiliency, initiative and optimism. A woman who possesses little of these important attributes will feel great levels of frustration, anxiety, fear and anger. One possible solution is to gain a greater awareness of her emotions, and then find ways to address these emotional needs so that her ability to adjust and bounce back are increased.

Emotional intelligence is a cornerstone to greater resiliency, and greater resiliency leads to stronger personal power and more serenity.

The five competencies of emotional intelligence are: self-awareness, self-management, self-motivation, recognizing emotions in others and empathizing, and one's ability to manage and nurture relationships with others. Every woman's level of emotional intelligence can be improved because this is all about behavior, and behavior is something that can be learned. Monitor your emotional state when in various situations and make the appropriate attitudinal shifts. Learn to understand and accept your emotions, and most of all learn how to balance them in various situations.

Improving your emotional intelligence can help you to better control you reaction to things that occur all around you. Additionally, controlling your emotions is better for your autonomic nervous system which is said to regulate 90% of our body functions, including the heart, brain, immune, hormonal, respiration and digestive systems. Imbalances in our autonomic nervous systems have been linked to panic disorder, anxiety disorder, sleep disorders, asthma, migraines, depression, dizziness, nausea, hypertension, sudden cardiac death, chronic fatigue, irritable bowel syndrome and premenstrual syndrome. When a woman has little control over her emotional state, the amount of the hormone cortisol released into the body increases. Cortisol has been found to cause a number of health-related problems.

Finding personal strategies to get more in-tune with your emotions not only can help you feel more in control, strong emotional intelligence can propel you up the ladder to life and work success. Get better acquainted with the range of your emotions and then identify effective strategies to control them. Your health and well-being depend upon your becoming emotionally intelligent.

Closing Thoughts

Are you suffering from inner kill? Are you blocking your own success and happiness? This is your life and it can become whatever you decide to make it. Someone, no one knows who for sure wrote:

> Life is a gift…Accept it
> Life is an adventure…Dare it
> Life is a mystery…Unfold it
> Life is a game…Play It
> Life is a struggle… Face It
> Life is beauty…Praise It
> Life is a puzzle.. Solve It
> Life is an opportunity…Take It
> Life is sorrowful…Experience It
> Life is a song…Sing It
> Life is a goal. Achieve It
> Life is a mission…Fulfill It

I have faced so many different challenges and problems in my life, but through sheer grit, determination and buckets of tears, I have been able to overcome them somehow, and still keep my sanity. Although some of my days have been tough and I was far from certain how I would make it through the horrific storms that swirled around me, I was thankful each time I was successfully able to solve a problem, meet a challenge, or grow stronger.

My faith in the Creator has grown over the years through these personal tests. The confidence I have in my ability to withstand the trials and tribulations of life has increased. I now know that no matter how dismal a situation may seem, I can survive, even thrive in spite of it all.

Once a woman stops and considers all that she has faced, all that she has been able to overcome, and acknowledges all that she has been able to accomplish, she becomes fully aware of her ability to persist toward a goal. She has begun to live soulfully.

When I have been overwhelmed with pain, agony and despair, I simply find a quiet place and sit still. When I have a tough decision to make or an obstacle to resolve, I listen intently to my spirit and take counsel with my heart and my mind. The bottom line is that whatever you face, if you sincerely believe that you can prevail, you will.

Every woman can learn to live a more fulfilling life by consciously deciding to seek more joy; by striving to use and live her life in a meaningful way.

A woman, who is self-aware, finds her calling, creates goals to achieve her calling, persists un-relentlessly, and chooses to maintain a positive attitude. As she brims with optimism each day, she is certain to experience more fulfillment in her life.

The journey to soulful living begins and ends one day at a time. Enjoy your special journey and always remember to keep counsel with your soul.

A Strong Woman Versus A Woman Of Strength
(*Anonymous*)

A strong woman works out every day to keep her body in shape…
But a woman of strength builds relationships to keep her soul in shape.

A strong woman isn't afraid of anything…
But a woman of strength shows courage in the midst of her fear.

A strong woman won't let anyone get the best of her…
But a woman of strength gives the best of herself to everyone.

A strong woman makes mistakes and avoids the same in the future…
But a woman of strength realizes life's mistakes can also be unexpected blessings and capitalizes on them.

A strong woman wears the look of confidence on her face…
But a woman of strength wears grace.

A strong woman has faith that she is strong enough for the journey…
But a woman of strength has faith that it is in the journey that she will become strong.

Pass this on to a woman of strength…I just did.

Good Fortune   Understanding

A Recipe for Soulful Living

Anita Davis-DeFoe

Start with one cup of talent, and three cups of gifts,
Blend in a heap of goals, and add a good attitude to this.

Stir in seven tablespoons of dreams, a cup of good habits and a dash of belief,
A few more ingredients and the recipe will be complete.

Add an ounce of purpose, and some resilience too,
Mix in a tablespoon of vision, sauté these ingredients just for a few.

Combine a half-cup of persistence, with a hint of passion sweet,
Together, personal passion, purpose and persistence will make this recipe unique.

Toss in a pinch of gingered hope, some love and a hint of fresh faith,
Pour in two pints of focus and a quart of determination according to taste.

You need to add a pound of courage, a cup of forgiveness, maybe two,
Shake in a gallon of spirit,
a bit of soul seasoning ads gusto to this wonderful life stew.

Simmer all of the ingredients and be sure not to boil,
Remember that to achieve anything in this life, there will be some toil.

Anything you mentally conceive, you can most definitely achieve,
Everything first begins as a vision, a quest; a precious dream.

Fill your plate; enjoy this dish, your hearty life stew,
Let it guide, empower and nourish, all that you do.

0-595-34240-X

Printed in the United States
26663LVS00003B/196-234